Praise for *THINK like a Nurse!*

"Nursing school has limitations to what can be taught before you graduate and enter the profession. *THINK like a Nurse!* addresses this and provides the new nurse with need to know content, along with Keith's clinical pearls, to help you see the 'big picture' of patient care. I strongly recommend this invaluable book for all nursing students and/or new graduates."

Andrea Baland, RN

Normandale Community College graduate, 2012

Bloomington, Minnesota

"This is a must read for all nursing students and new graduates. The content is invaluable and will encourage you to live up to your full potential as a new nurse!"

Desiree Rohling, RN

Normandale Community College graduate, 2012

Bloomington, Minnesota

"After reading this book, I am more confident to go into my nursing practice. The wealth of practical information in this short read is like having a year's worth of nursing experience under my belt. I highly recommend this valuable book for new grads!"

Tamera Wimbley, RN

Normandale Community College graduate, 2013

Bloomington, Minnesota

"Keith has the insight for the conceptual framework in teaching young nurses. This book provides many examples to help student nurses and new graduates filter the crucial aspects of caring for their patient's and the patient's family."

Georgia Hogenson, PhD, RN, CNOR

Assistant Professor

Department of Nursing

College of St. Benedict/St. John's University

St. Joseph, Minnesota

"I highly recommend *THINK like a Nurse!* This book is perfect for student nurses in the last semester of their nursing program and for new graduate nurses. Keith takes the common core knowledge and skills that the new nurse needs and drills them down to the nuggets of wisdom needed to be successful in practice. His thoughts and experiences in practice are insightful and easy to apply. A great resource for nurse educators too!"

Melinda M. Luther, MS, RN, CNE
Professor and Chair
Department of Nursing
Nashua Community College
Nashua, New Hampshire

"THINK like a Nurse! provides relevant information in an easy-to-read, clear, and focused manner along with helpful advice from an expert nurse and teacher. This practical information is integrated with important professional issues and content such as civility, QSEN, the ANA Code of Ethics, and providing safe and holistic patient-centered care. I believe this book is a powerful resource for nursing students. They can read/review this book each semester and subsequently improve their ability to "think like a nurse" with each clinical experience as they progress through their nursing program and even their first year of nursing practice."

Shirlee J. Snyder, EdD, RN
Interim Dean and Professor
School of Nursing
Nevada State College
Henderson, Nevada

THINK like a Nurse!

Practical Preparation for Professional Practice

Author: Keith Rischer, RN, MA, CEN, CCRN

Copyright © 2013 by Keith Rischer
ISBN: 978-0-9899369-0-3

All rights reserved. No part of this publication may be reproduced or transmitted in any form or by any means, electronic or mechanical, including photocopy, recording, or any information storage and retrieval system, without the prior written permission of the author.

To request a review copy for course adoption, or to inquire regarding speaker availability; email Keith:
Keith@KeithRN.com

Dedication

This book is warmly dedicated to Patricia Benner, RN, PhD, FAAN, FRCN and her ongoing influence to leave the profession of nursing better than when she entered it. Her work as an educator, author, researcher, and scholar has impacted the nursing profession in this generation as well as my own practice as a clinician and educator. It is my desire to honor and practically situate her work that spans over thirty years for the next generation of caregivers in this book. Her emphasis on the importance of caring as well as clinical reasoning and thinking like a nurse in practice makes her work timeless and relevant to all participants in the nursing profession today.

Acknowledgements

This book has truly been a team project. Though I had an idea of what I wanted to communicate when I started this project a few months ago, it was truly a diamond in the ROUGH. But with the input and suggestions of many respected educators and nurses in clinical practice it has become better and more "polished" as a result. I would like to give special mention to the following out of my appreciation for their contributions:

A heartfelt thank-you to Patricia Benner, RN, PhD, FAAN, FRCN for her willingness to read an early draft as well as final draft of this manuscript and provide needed global feedback. Your assistance in helping me rescue the "house" metaphor with a vibrant, living house that is *"dynamic, changing and growing to better fit a growing practice...making the home more of a peaceful and healing abode, for yourself, and for the patient"* was needed and appreciated!

A special thanks to Cynthia Clark, RN, PhD, ANEF, FAAN whose research work on incivility is extensive in the literature. You demonstrated to me what civility looks like as well as professional collegiality through your willingness to take time out of your busy schedule to review the appendix on incivility and provide needed feedback and revision.

I also want to thank Linda Caputi, MSN, EdD, RN, CNE for her part in opening the doors that gave me the opportunity to present my work on clinical reasoning as an unknown educator on a national stage at Elsevier's Faculty Development Institute two years ago. I was so nervous I almost passed out before I spoke, but I got through it and would not have this platform today had it not been for you! You too, took time out of your busy schedule to review this manuscript. I appreciate your honest and direct feedback to refine what I communicate in this book.

I also had reviewers who went through this manuscript with a fine-toothed comb. I am so thankful to Melinda Luther, MS, RN, CNE, department chair at Nashua Community College in New Hampshire. Your willingness to contribute to this manuscript was a blessing. We share the same passion in our approach to nursing, and your contributions and encouragement were needed and appreciated!

I am also grateful to Georgia Dinndorf-Hogenson, PhD, RN, CNOR who also thoroughly reviewed this manuscript. Your commitment to educational excellence has been an inspiration and encouragement to me. You have been a friend and colleague through both thick and thin in academia!

A special thank you to Ruby Wertz, MSHA, BSN, RN who took my manuscript on vacation to provide needed input. I also appreciate your kindness and collegiality to make my first nursing department presentation a success at Nevada State College!

Another heart-felt thank you to Shirlee J. Snyder EdD, RN who provided a final review of my manuscript. After all my feedback had been incorporated into the draft, I needed one final set of eyes who was a nurse editor and author. Despite being in the middle of revising your fundamentals nursing textbook (Kozier and Erb's) you took the time to provide final revisions and edits. Your validation of what I have written has given me peace of mind to finalize this manuscript and publish!

Thank you Kari Ryan, RN, BAN, a staff nurse at Abbott Northwestern where I practice. You are an inspiration to me whose heart remains engaged and caring. You are a real-life example that demonstrates that after thirty years at the bedside you can still remain fresh and alive in practice. Your comments and input to the draft contributed to the "living house" metaphor by your example.

I have been blessed and thankful to have two editors, Jan Leisner, MA, and Rosalie Krusemark who have improved and polished my original manuscript. Your input and attention to the smallest detail has made this book the best it can possibly be. You both were willing to work with a tight schedule and I appreciate your flexibility to complete this project!

I want to thank my former nursing students Heather Squillacioti, Jennifer Shipsted, Desiree Rohling, Andrea Baland and Tamera Wimbley, now new nurses in practice, who reviewed this manuscript and provided clarifications and revisions based on their perspective as a new nurse to improve its relevance to my primary audience.

I am indebted and want to thank the nursing students at Normandale Community College class of 2012 who were my "guinea pigs" as I went outside the box of traditional nursing education to do my best to implement the suggestions of Patricia Benner and her coauthors in *Educating Nurses*. You recognized the value of what I was trying to accomplish. This book and the opportunities I now have to present clinical reasoning across the country would not have been possible if not for you!

Finally, it goes without being said that behind every good man is a better woman, and that woman is my wife, Rhonda. I am so thankful for your practical day to day support and willingness to sacrifice so that I could complete my masters in nursing education and pursue my passion as a nurse educator.

Table of Contents

Author's Preface

Foreword

Introduction

Part I: Building the "Living" House of Professional Practice

Chapter 1: Foundation: The "Art" of Nursing

Chapter 2: The Walls: Applied Sciences

Chapter 3: The Roof: Thinking Like a Nurse

Chapter 4: Supporting Structures: Safety, Education, & Expert Practice

Part II: Practical Preparation for Practice

Chapter 5: Putting It All Together: Clinical Reasoning Case Studies
- Sepsis: Unfolding Clinical Reasoning Case Study

Chapter 6: Clinical Pearls

Chapter 7: Clinical Wisdom from Nurses in Practice

Appendices:
- A. Skeletons in the Closet: Nurse-to-Nurse Bullying and Incivility
- B. Skeletons in the Closet: Men in Nursing
- C. Practical Preparation to Pass the NCLEX
- D. Worksheet: Medications That Must Be Mastered
- E. Worksheet: Laboratory Tests That Must Be Mastered
- F. Worksheet: Patient Preparation
- G. Handout: Clinical Lab Values and Nursing Responsibilities
- H. Handout: Most Commonly Used Categories of Medications
- I. Handout: Comprehending Cardiac Medications
- J. Handout: Clinical Reasoning Questions to Develop Nurse Thinking
- K. Clinical Reasoning Resources and KeithRN
- L. Medical Missions and Faith-Based Resources

References

Author's Preface

Every Book Has a Story…This Is My Story

Lights and sirens blazing, I was the emergency medical technician (EMT) and driver of an ambulance racing to the scene of a 9-1-1 call for chest pain. The paramedic was in the back of the ambulance with the patient who was receiving needed care. We were on a back country road in the days before GPS. All I had was a Hudson's map book to get me back to the main highway. I took a wrong turn, got lost, and began to panic! After some quick thinking, I finally found the way back to the main road and made it back to the emergency department (ED), but not before the family beat our rig to the hospital! Fortunately the patient was not impacted by the delay, but this caused me to reflect and realize that I needed to reconsider my suitability for emergency services!

What attracted me to nursing over thirty years ago was caring in crisis, in the context of emergency care. I wanted to be a flight nurse/paramedic and chose to get my nursing degree right out of high school. I completed my EMT after my first year of nursing school and began to volunteer as an EMT in our community. I was so traumatized by getting lost with a patient in the ambulance, that I re-routed my career path and completed my two-year nursing degree in 1983 from a local community college and entered a very tight job market as a registered nurse.

I started my nursing career as a psychiatric nurse at the local state hospital and had to slowly stair step from there to pursue my ongoing desire for caring in crisis: long-term care, pediatric home care, step-down NICU, cardiac telemetry, cardiac ICU, and finally after sixteen years, the ED. I currently work in the critical care float pool of a large metro hospital where I work between the ED, med/surg neuro ICU, cardiac medical ICU, cardiac surgical ICU, cardiac telemetry and circulating/rapid response team. I am relatively new to nursing education, having taught several years as a clinical adjunct and only two years full-time in the classroom.

My journey in nursing education began on a medical mission trip to Honduras nine years ago. Our team served at a mission hospital in a rural underserved community. They had multiple physicians and a surgeon, but no one to deliver anesthesia on a consistent basis. The hospital was dependent on medical teams that had a certified registered nurse anesthetist (CRNA). Only then did they have the ability to do major surgery. I was helping in the OR that day and no CRNA was available. Instead of general anesthesia, I was titrating Ketamine as an IV push for a child having minor abdominal surgery correcting a hernia. Ketamine is a dissociative anesthetic that is used for conscious sedation, NOT a general anesthetic. We did the best we could under the circumstances, but during the procedure it was obvious he was in discomfort and would become restless as the sedation lightened up. After this experience I was determined to obtain my CRNA and do what I could to make a difference and serve in this context in medical mission work in the future.

I had current ICU experience, but only a two-year nursing degree so I enrolled in a local BSN completion program, completed my BSN and then applied at a local CRNA school. At this point I thought it would be wise to see firsthand what a CRNA does in practice and shadowed a nurse anesthetist for a day. I was totally disillusioned! This role was not what I expected; I was BORED by this experience at the end of the day! One of my favorite ways to relax and unwind is with a good book. I was reading *Wild at Heart* a book by John Eldredge that encourages men to recapture their uniquely created heart that is wired for adventure. This quote literally jumped off the page:

"Don't ask yourself what the world needs. Ask yourself what makes you come alive, and do that. Because what the world needs are people who have come fully alive" *(1)*.

I realized how much I enjoyed teaching new nurses in the ED. I enjoyed seeing what I was teaching and presenting, watching the "light bulb" turn on as content was understood and incorporated into practice by other nurses. This quote gave me permission to pursue what I believe is my God-given passion and talent in nursing, the ability to teach. So after completing my BSN, instead of pursuing the path of what was NEEDED as a CRNA, I pursued my PASSION and went right to a master's in nursing education program and have not looked back!

Trouble in Paradise

After my second year of classroom teaching in 2010, I began to feel a disconnect and was dissatisfied. I knew what content was needed and relevant for students as a nurse straddling both domains of education and clinical practice. Between the traditional content-heavy lectures and North American Nursing Diagnosis Association (NANDA) driven care plans with a correctly worded three part nursing diagnostic statement, I felt this traditional approach was not fully preparing my students to think like a nurse in clinical practice. Everything changed when I read *Educating Nurses: A Call for Radical Transformation* over winter break written by Patricia Benner and her co-authors. The recommendations for nurse educators was founded on educational research findings by the Carnegie Foundation (their findings are not limited to the nursing profession) and identified that nursing education needed to be TRANSFORMED by the following "radical" proposals:

- CONTEXTUALIZE classroom content so it is situated in clinical practice (at the bedside) so students can see why it is relevant.

- Greater INTEGRATION of classroom theory and clinical content so that they are not kept in largely separate orbits in nursing education.
- Emphasize CINICAL REASONING, which is the ability of the nurse to think in action and reason as a situation changes over time by capturing and understanding the significance of clinical trajectories and grasping the essence of the current clinical situation (2).

In a nutshell, all that is taught in the classroom must translate to the BEDSIDE! This captured so concisely in writing what I was feeling inside that I knew it demanded a response and I had to do something different, and fast! So I spent the last half of my winter break reworking my assigned theory content so that my lectures would incorporate and apply these paradigm changes in my classroom. I was determined to be the change! I had all of the cardiac content that semester and situated my four content lectures on "Mr. Kelly," a middle-aged/overweight man who developed at the beginning of lecture #1 Atherosclerosis/HTN and for lecture #2 progressed to AMI, in lecture #3 he developed heart failure, and in lecture #4 his cardiac disease progressed to PAD/PVD. I cut my lecture content in half by emphasizing CONCEPTS and used the other half to situate student learning through a clinical reasoning case study that I created by incorporating the best aspects from Lisa Day's paradigm example from *Educating Nurses* and Linda Caputi's clinical reasoning activities as well as my own clinical experience. I required students to identify RELEVANT data and establish nursing priorities/interventions with a clinical scenario using clinical reasoning. I developed my own template of a clinical reasoning case study and used this to situate all of my lecture content for the semester.

I did a simple survey at the end of the semester to see what student's thought of this new approach to nursing education. Student response afterward was overwhelmingly positive. NOT ONE student said to go back to traditional content-heavy lectures but continue this emphasis on need-to-know concepts and clinical reasoning using case studies in the classroom! One student summed it up for many: *"These clinical reasoning case studies were very helpful. I didn't feel like I was memorizing for the test. I felt like I was able to apply the information. It helped put knowledge into practice and made it clear why it was relevant."*

After I had successfully adapted this needed emphasis of clinical reasoning in my classroom, I had a chance encounter with a nationally known nurse educator and long-time advocate of clinical reasoning, Linda Caputi. Unknown to me at the time, she was also on the planning committee of a large, annual national nurse educators conference (Elsevier's Faculty Development Institute). She was interested in what I had developed, and after reviewing my case studies I was invited to speak and share my work on how I adapted clinical reasoning and the paradigm changes from *Educating Nurses* in a well-received breakout session

I realized that many other nurse educators also recognized the need to do something very different to promote the learning of their students. Though many had read *Educating Nurses*, the practical application of HOW to make this transformation possible was not so clear. Knowing that there was an ongoing interest in this needed emphasis of clinical reasoning resources, over the past year I took the initiative to develop and build my website KeithRN. KeithRN has numerous resources to develop nurse thinking as well as clinical reasoning case studies that I charge a small fee for on a wide variety of med/surg topics derived from my many years of clinical practice. Much of what I have developed and posted are FREE downloads including clinical handouts and the templates to build your own clinical reasoning case studies if you are a nurse educator. It is my desire to share with other faculty what I have developed so that this needed transformation can be facilitated!

In the past year, numerous students began to access the clinical reasoning resources on my website, even purchasing case studies to help promote their learning. I realized that they too wanted to benefit from this needed emphasis on clinical reasoning. This book was birthed by this desire to promote their learning and understanding of clinical reasoning. I have put in writing what I have taught to my students over the years as well as what I have presented at national and regional nurse educator conferences. I consider myself an "everyday educator" who is no scholar, but grounded in clinical practice. I possess a heartfelt desire to do what I can to promote the learning of those who also want to pursue their passion to become a nurse. I also want to do what I can to be a part of the needed transformation that is currently needed in nursing education to better prepare our nurses for real-world practice.

Foreword

As a student, I have known Keith from my first year of nursing school; he was one of my fundamental nursing instructors, who is now a nursing colleague in the float pool at the hospital we both work at. Keith's passion for nursing is evident not only in his practice at the bedside but also through his teaching. The clinical reasoning case studies that he created and presented to our class challenged us to think in a way that we had not experienced to this point in nursing school. His objective was to get us to "think" like a nurse. As his students in lecture, we had to take a step back and look at the bigger picture of what was truly going on with the patient in the clinical scenario. As a class we had to identify what the clinical data represented and as nurses what interventions we should implement to intervene and prevent a worst possible scenario from happening. Keith was constantly challenging and encouraging us.

Keith had faith in us, and laid a foundation of knowledge that was applied at the bedside. Keith pushed us to start utilizing the same clinical reasoning questions during clinical. Not only did this prepare us before caring for our patients, but it also helped us to be more proficient and consistent with our skills. On a personal level, Keith cares. He was present during a crisis in my life during nursing school. He not only showed compassion for my situation and care as a friend, but his knowledge and grasp of nursing was evident.

This book has been extremely helpful to me in many ways. Not only did it remind me of all the clinical handouts Keith created that I relied on during clinical (i.e., most commonly used medication, clinical reasoning questions, etc.), but also reminded me of the living "house" nursing represents…the foundation, walls, and roof. Keith also reminded us of the centrality of caring to nursing. The content in chapter 1 on the foundation of nursing must be carefully read and not overlooked or missed by the reader. Keith goes into further detail on how to pull what we have learned from the classroom and apply it to the bedside, and how trending data is essential in practice. Chapter 6 uncovers the clinical pearls that are relevant to practice is something every new graduate entering the workforce should review and apply. The appendix on bullying is a must read as well. I highly recommend this book to be read by new graduate nurses and applied at the bedside to help prepare you for practice.

Heather Squillacioti, RN
Normandale Community College graduate, 2012
Abbott Northwestern Hospital, Float Pool
Minneapolis, Minnesota

Introduction

I have written this book to help you as a new nurse transition successfully and not only survive but THRIVE in clinical practice! This book is filled with relevant information that will help facilitate your professional growth as a new nurse. This book was written specifically for the new nurse or graduate nurse who is either waiting to take the NCLEX or has passed and is now pursuing that first job to begin your nursing career. But this book will also benefit any nursing student, even at the fundamental level. It will be pertinent because if you review the content in this book each semester, you will learn something new based on your previous clinical experiences and higher level theory content. I have put my thoughts in writing, but more importantly have highlighted the writings of leading nurse educators such as Patricia Benner, who will mentor and guide you as you begin your lifelong journey of learning as a student or graduate nurse.

I love the energy and passion that nursing students bring into the classroom and clinical settings to promote their learning. They are engaged, focused, and have willingly made numerous sacrifices to make it through nursing school. If you are a graduating nurse, I warmly congratulate you! I know that you desire to be the best nurse you can be to provide safe care for your patients. But with great power of learning comes great responsibility. Are you at times fearful or anxious over the reality that you will soon be fully responsible for all aspects of your patient's care…that you literally hold a human life in your hands? If you can identify with this roller coaster of emotions as you prepare for professional practice, I have written this book with you in mind.

You will never stop learning as a professional nurse. As a graduate nurse you have an excellent foundation laid from your education, but you are likely feeling the burn of your own fears and anxieties as you transition to autonomous professional practice. "Reality shock" is just around the corner for you as a graduate nurse. The differences between your academic environment and the values you were taught are going to collide with the clinical culture you will practice in. Extremely high levels of stress, anxiety, burnout, and turnover are common for the new nurse in the first year of practice (1). Many new graduate nurses leave the profession in the first year because of job stress, lack of organizational support, poor nurse-physician relations, unreasonable workloads, uncivil work environments, and difficulty transitioning to practice (2).

To prepare you for real world practice, this book will highlight content areas most relevant to the bedside and why they must be mastered and understood. I have chosen to capitalize words throughout the book for emphasis of importance (not to yell!). To help visualize the professional development that is needed as you transition to the responsibilities of the professional nurse, I will use the metaphor of building a house; not a static structure, but a unique, vibrant "living" house that is a reflection of how you choose to build and add to it over time. Nursing is a living and vibrant practice that requires your personal involvement and engagement to promote the well-being of those you care for. Just as a home often undergoes remodeling as a family grows over time, the same is true for the professional nurse who may change practice settings or advance their education to "remodel" their practice setting to management, education, or nurse anesthesia. The "living" house of professional practice will be developed in the following chapters of this book.

A house must have a firm and stable foundation. The ethical comportment or the art of nursing is this foundation for every nurse. Caring behaviors, nurse engagement, and professionalism in practice must be present or your nursing practice could be on shaky ground before it even begins. Once the foundation is laid it is time to build, and the walls of professional practice are the applied sciences of nursing: pharmacology, fluid and electrolytes, and anatomy and physiology. I will contextualize these essential sciences to the bedside so you can see the relevance of mastering this content and therefore enhance your ability to recognize potentially dangerous clinical trends and provide the best possible care for your patients. Finally, the roof of professional practice consists of critical thinking and clinical reasoning, which is the thinking that is required by the nurse that completes the house and ties everything together.

Though most students can write a three part nursing diagnostic statement and use this as a priority for a written care plan, this emphasis will not always prepare you to transition to thinking like a nurse in practice. As a nurse in practice, you must be able to THINK IN ACTION especially when the status of your patient changes. This is the essence of clinical reasoning and is an essential thinking skill that must be understood, incorporated, and practiced.

The house of professional practice is in need of supporting structures that include safety, education, and expert practice. Safety is practically situated in all that a nurse does at the bedside. The nurse must also embrace the role of educator and realize how patient education can positively impact patient outcomes and even prevent readmissions. Though it takes time to progress to expert practice, what it takes to get there will be identified so that you can be the best that you were trained and created to be!

Finally, we will tie the house together with real world clinical scenarios to apply all that you have learned in this book as well as your nursing education. You will be able to practice clinical reasoning by using the unfolding clinical reasoning case study on sepsis found in chapter five and by accessing the unique clinical reasoning case studies found on my website KeithRN.com/, which situate foundational concepts and content for practice. Each case study has a fully developed answer key that thoroughly explains the rationale to promote your learning. This allows you to PRACTICE nurse thinking before you enter into practice.

I have compiled essential and relevant clinical pearls that will practically guide you in the clinical setting. The final chapter is filled with rich pearls of wisdom from nurses that I work with in acute care and what they would say to you, the next generation of nurses, to be practically prepared for professional practice. In every house there are also closets, and unfortunately there are two "skeletons in the closet" that are identified and discussed at length in appendix A and B. The remaining appendices contain several of the clinical handouts I have created to promote the learning of my students.

Acute care positions in a hospital setting have traditionally been the most common and desired clinical practice areas for nurses. But now more than half of all nursing positions are found in other settings including home care, transitional care units (TCU) and long-term care and this is where many of you will begin your career. Nursing is so much more than acute care in the hospital setting! The majority of my nursing career has been acute care in a hospital setting. This is my lens and the framework that I use in my nursing practice and is the clinical context for much of this book. I am confident that you will still find the content in this book meaningful and relevant to promote your professional development regardless of your practice setting.

It is only recently that I pursued my passion to teach and became a nurse educator. I care deeply about your professional success and want to do what I can to establish you on a rock-solid foundation as you transition to professional practice. One of my greatest frustrations as a nurse educator has been the inherent difficulty of sharing the depth of my clinical experience with my students because I have been spread so thin as a clinical educator. Though I enjoy the dynamics of clinical education, I feel like a ping pong ball bouncing from one "crisis" to the next. So now that you have the time and I have put my thoughts in writing, I invite you to pull up a chair and let me share what will help you to be practically prepared for professional practice.

Additional Resources:

- Book: *From Surviving to Thriving: Navigating the First Year of Professional Practice* by Judy Boychuk Duchscher

- Book: *A Daybook for Beginning Nurses* by Donna Wilk Cardillo

- Book: *Your First Year As a Nurse, Making the Transition from Total Novice to Successful Professional*, 2nd edition by Donna Wilk Cardillo

Part I: Building the "Living" House of Professional Practice

Chapter 1: Foundation: The "Art" of Nursing

Do You Care?

The foundation matters. Build your home on sand or unsteady soil, and all the hard work of what you have built will someday come crashing down. Build your house on a rock solid foundation and it will withstand any storm and last a lifetime. You will experience a multitude of storms in professional practice, especially in the first year! How you lay and build your foundation is the most important aspect of the living house of professional practice. The "art" of nursing is the foundation of nursing practice and consists of caring, compassion, nurse engagement, and professional behaviors. This is why it is so important to reflect and see if these foundational aspects of professional practice are present in you or need to be strengthened. These essential components make the house of professional practice unique as a vibrant and living home. It represents your heart and internal motivations to serve and care for others. If you lack empathetic caring, your practice will reflect this and will be devoid of life. But if you are truly caring and engaged you will bring life to everyone you touch by your caring presence!

Caring has traditionally been viewed as the essence of nursing practice and the most important characteristic of a nurse (1). Caring is also a distinct, dominant, central, and unifying focus for nursing practice (2). Caring as a recognized core value in nursing is not new, but was emphasized at the beginning of the modern era by influential nurse educator Isabel Hampton Robb, who later went on to found the American Nurses Association in 1897. In 1900, she wrote in her textbook *Nursing Ethics:*

The spirit in which she does her work makes all the difference. Invested as she should with the dignity of her profession and the cloak of love for suffering humanity, she can ennoble anything her hand may be called upon to do, and for work done in this spirit there will ever come to her a recompense far outweighing that of silver and gold (3).

While Hampton Robb stated in the language of her day that nurses should provide care by embracing "the dignity of her profession and the cloak of love for suffering humanity" it is important to recognize that this must NOT be treated as a philosophical abstract platitude. This must be embraced by the nurse as a philosophical TRUTH that must be LIVED OUT in how you care for others (4). You will be caring for real people who have intrinsic worth regardless of the quality of life decisions they have made that may have contributed to their need for care. Therefore the nurse must meet and care for the patient as a valued person whom you share a common humanity with. The essence of caring as a nurse is that you recognize the value and worth of those you care for and that the patient and their experience MATTER to you (5).

Though the emphasis in nursing education is primarily knowledge acquisition and skill development, this in itself is not enough; you must CARE and have COMPASSION for others. Patricia Benner also affirms that caring is central to nursing practice. *"Nursing can never be reduced to mere technique…the nature of the caring relationship is central to most nursing interventions"* (5, p.4). *"The nurse is both a knowledge worker and one who cares…knowledge is dangerous if it is divorced from caring"* (5, p.400). This is the unique legacy of the nursing profession throughout history including the modern era ushered in by Nightingale.

The nurse must make a decision to "go there" to care, but when you give of yourself in this way to care for your patients, it touches you in a special way and you receive a "recompense far outweighing that of silver and gold" (3). Though I try to make this principle a part of my practice, I am inconsistent and often allow the "tyranny of the urgent" to distract me from this ideal. But I had a recent clinical example that hit home and made it clear how important this is to nursing practice.

I recently had a very busy shift in the ED with numerous demands, being pulled in all too many directions at the same time. One of my patients was a healthy middle-aged man who had numerous vague respiratory complaints the past week including shortness of breath. The physician ordered a chest X-ray and numerous tumors were found in both lung fields. Because a full workup is not done in the ED, the physician explained that it was likely cancer with a poor prognosis, but he required hospital admission to complete a full workup. I went into the room fifteen minutes later and found the patient had tears in his eyes, realizing that his world would never be the same. I did not know what to say, except that I was so sorry, and then had to leave due to the admitting physician who came and needed to assess him.

I called report to the receiving nurse, and transport came to take the patient to the floor. I wanted to share some encouraging words that were heavy on my own heart before he left the ED, but when I went to his room he was gone. Though he was a stranger, his experience and what he was feeling really did matter to me. Though it would have been easy to forget it, and move on to deal with the next crisis, I could not shake the clear impression to visit him before I left for home at the end of my shift. I punched out, and went to his room on the oncology floor. He lit up when he saw me as I entered. I briefly shared what was on my heart. With tears in his eyes he said something I will never forget. *"Your decision to come and see me is special, and it makes me feel special because you care."* Though this patient was clearly touched, it also fueled my tank of caring to see how I was used to make a difference to this patient. Though this is my story, you can have a similar one as the story of those you care for matter to you.

Caring is not without risk because if you care, you become vulnerable, experience stress and personal concern. Many nurses then allow the pendulum to swing the other way and become detached and disengaged in practice. If you remain disengaged in practice you are more likely NOT to recognize relevant data and act upon it to rescue your patient when there is a change in status (6).

A challenge you will experience when caring for your patients will be the incredible diversity and lived experiences of those you care for. In addition to the obvious ethnic and cultural diversity, you will care for patients who may have an addiction to narcotics, alcohol or other substances. Some may be verbally abusive, sexually suggestive and provocative in their behavior. Will you care then? Though abusive behavior must never be tolerated, it is important to step back, try to understand the lived experience of your patient and what may have contributed to the person you are now caring for today (5). To authentically care for those that are not easy to care for requires a balanced approach from the nurse. The balance comes by remaining engaged, understanding the patient's situation, having a heart filled with compassion and remaining patient-centered in all that you do.

Patient-Centered Care

When the nurse begins to UNDERSTAND how the patient's current illness has impacted his life and those around him, this provides the lens to see from his context and is foundational to empathetic caring and patient-centered care. This allows the nurse to not just react, but INTERPRET the current situation (5). For example, if you go into the patient's room and he states angrily, "Can't you just leave me alone! I am so tired of being messed with!" Instead of reacting to this outburst and taking it personally, knowing he was recently diagnosed with stage IV pancreatic cancer and has three months to live will provide contextual interpretation to remain engaged and present in his care.

The value of Patient-centered care is also emphasized and is the first competency of the Quality and Safety Education for Nurses (QSEN). The goal of QSEN "*is to address the challenge of preparing future nurses with the knowledge, skills, and attitudes necessary to continuously improve the quality and safety of the healthcare systems in which they work*" (7). Many of you have been exposed to QSEN in nursing education and QSEN remains relevant in clinical practice. QSEN defines and complements what we have already discussed by its recognition that patient-centered care happens when the nurse "*recognizes the patient or designee as the source of control and full partner in providing COMPASSIONATE and coordinated care based on respect for patient's preferences, values, and needs*" (7). The underlying attitudes that are required by the nurse to provide patient centered care according to QSEN include seeing health-care situations through the patient's eyes, respect, encourage individual expression of what the patient needs, and value active partnership with the patient and family in all aspects of care (7).

Benefits of Caring

Caring gives you a heightened sense of awareness and guides the evaluation of nursing interventions by recognizing subtle changes in your patient's condition. In this context of caring, the nurse is paying close attention to the patient's body language, facial expressions, tone of voice and interpreting the significance of what is being communicated (5). When your head and heart are integrated and engaged in practice, you clearly communicate in both verbal and non-verbal communication that each person matters. Patients can readily detect a nurse's non-verbal communication. Recognize the influence and significance of your eye contact, body language, and tone of voice when you interact with your patient and how these can communicate caring and contribute to a patient's well-being (5).

Caring behaviors also create healing environments that positively influence and improve patient outcomes. The benefits patients receive when they experience caring by the nurse include: enhanced healing, decreased length of stay, increased well-being and physical comfort. When patients do not feel cared for, the emotional consequences include feelings of being frightened, out of control, helplessness, and vulnerability (6). Practicing in a caring manner also benefits the nurse and leads to the nurse's well-being, both personally and professionally. The nurse feels more connected both to his or her patients and colleagues and is more satisfied with bedside care (6).

Caring Made Practical

I have found the caring theory work of Kristen Swanson and her original research article "Empirical Development of a Middle Range Theory of Caring" helpful to identify themes of what constitutes and defines caring by the nurse. Swanson investigates what patients value and perceive as caring behaviors from their lens and perspective (8). I believe that caring is not rigid or static and must never be reduced to a set of behaviors or interventions performed by the nurse. It is best if the nurse utilizes these caring interventions as "tools in the toolbox" that can be incorporated depending on the unique needs of the patient and their present circumstances.

In "Caring Made Visible" Swanson further explains her caring theory so that it is easily understood. For example, two relevant caring interventions identified by Swanson are "conveying availability" and "avoiding assumptions". When the nurse "conveys availability", this demonstrates caring (8). So instead of saying to your patient, *"Here is the call-light"*, you can state, *"Here is the call-light; do not hesitate to call me. I am available if you need me."*

"Avoiding assumptions" stresses the importance of the nurse to not rely upon another nurse's judgments about the patient, but to make your own assumptions by approaching the patient with a "clean slate" (8). When a nurse makes a preconceived judgment he/she ceases to be able to demonstrate caring. I have experienced this challenge personally when I practice in the ED where it is very easy to make judgments/assumptions with the unpleasant experiences other nurses may have had with a certain patient.

To practically situate these foundational components of nurse caring, I use two simple questions that can be used in clinical practice for each patient you care for:

1. What is the patient likely experiencing/feeling right now in this situation?

2. What can I do to engage myself with this patient's experience, and show that they matter to me as a person?

The way that you respond to each patient using these questions will vary. As you intentionally engage with each personal story, clinical situation, family dynamics, and culture/ethnic traditions, you will be well on your way to tailoring and providing the best possible care for your patient!

Comfort Theory

Though it may be obvious, continually monitoring and assessing the COMFORT of your patient will also demonstrate caring. Katherine Kolcaba, the author of "The Comfort Theory" proposes that COMFORT is a desirable holistic outcome that is central to nursing care. When patients have their comfort needs met, their well-being and personal needs are strengthened. Patient outcomes are improved when patient comfort needs are met (9). Comfort Theory provides a framework for the nurse to see comfort holistically and much more than just the relief of pain. Kolcaba defines COMFORT as "the immediate experience of being strengthened by having needs for relief, ease, and transcendence met in the following four contexts:

- Physical
    - Physical needs most commonly relating to pain control.
- Psycho-spiritual
    - Internal awareness of needs of self-esteem, sexuality, meaning of one's life and relationship to a higher order or being.
- Social
    - Awareness of the influence of family and other interpersonal relationships.
- Environmental
    - How external surroundings influence comfort (9).

Though relief of pain will always be central to providing comfort, open your eyes to see your patient holistically and provide comfort as able to these other spheres of your patient's being as well.

Caring for Families

Families and family members are as unique as the patients in your care. They can be friendly and supportive but can also be challenging, time-consuming, and demanding. The nurse must have a frame of reference that does not just tolerate families, but recognizes their value because they are an extension of the patient. Families also need information, reassurance, guidance, and CARE. For those with large families, make it a priority to identify the primary family spokesperson so that all health-related information goes to this person and prevents the nurse from receiving numerous phone calls for updates.

The importance of including the family in providing care is also emphasized throughout the QSEN competencies. Under the competency of Patient-centered Care, it is expected that the nurse will involve the FAMILY and identify their preferences and values, remove barriers to the presence of FAMILIES, elicit expectations of the patient AND FAMILY regarding relief of pain, value active partnership with patient AND FAMILY surrogates, examine how safety can be improved through the active involvement of patient AND FAMILIES, describe strategies to empower patients OR FAMILIES, and finally, assess level of communication skill in encounters with patients AND FAMILIES (7).

Remember that families are also under duress and need support by the nurse as well. Practical ways to support families include taking the time to update them in a non-hurried manner with what they need to know at their level of understanding, conveying availability by making it clear they can call anytime for an update, speaking in a gentle, respectful tone of voice, and involving them as much as possible in the care of the patient.

I have practically implemented some of these approaches by having family members use a moistened oral swab to moisten their mother's mouth while on a ventilator, or do simple hygiene such as combing her hair or giving their dad a shave. I have seen that when family needs are met and they are cared for, family members experience decreased anxiety and greater peace in the storm that they are currently going through. A recent example in my own practice highlights this point.

I cared for a patient in ICU who was critically ill, but beginning to make slow but steady progress. There were numerous pictures of Jesus on the wall of her room, and I asked the mother if faith was important to her daughter. She stated, "No, I brought these pictures for me. My daughter no longer goes to church, but I am praying daily and I know that God will work all things together for good." I acknowledged her feelings and stated that I too would pray for her daughter. Her face lit up with a big smile which said more than any words. The LITTLE things that are done in practice are in reality the BIG things that make a difference to support the families of those we care for.

Caring in Context

Why is caring and compassion so central to nursing and why does it remain so after over 2,000 years of caregiving history? In order to put this emphasis of caring into historical context there has always been a strong link between nursing and religious orders (10). From the first century to the Middle Ages, caring for the sick has been a ministry of the Christian church performed by both lay deacons and deaconesses and later through nun and monastery orders. To care for the sick was self-sacrificing in this era because exposure to diseases could be incurable and result in death (10). Showing compassion and caring for the sick was founded on the teachings and example of Jesus, who demonstrated high regard for human life through His model of service, sacrifice, and teaching that "in everything, do to others what you would have them do to you" (Mathew 7:12, English Standard Version).

Nightingale was also influenced by this same value system and her faith and belief in God motivated her to transform health-care and the nursing profession (11). At the age of seventeen, Nightingale felt that God had spoken to her and was calling her to service. As a young woman who sensed God leading her to devote herself to works of charity in hospitals, she recognized the need for healthcare training, but her parents were wealthy and respectable, and caring for the sick in England was anything but respectable! Nurses routinely came to work drunk, and immoral conduct was present even on the wards. Therefore she obtained her healthcare training at the moral and respectable Lutheran Deaconesses in Germany. She viewed nursing as a search for truth and used God's laws of healing in nursing practice (12). She willingly chose to sacrificially serve during the Crimean War caring for the wounded, making rounds as the "lady with the lamp," and educating nurses. She implemented numerous reforms to lower the 73 percent mortality rate from diseases alone and had a 1,000 page report of statistics she had compiled during this time. Nightingale established her schools of nursing after the war based on her "evidence-based practice" (13).

In reviewing fundamental textbooks on Florence Nightingale, I have found that many minimize or ignore the role of her faith as a motivating factor for her self-sacrificing service. This is relevant to you as a new nurse if you have similar influencing desires to enter the nursing profession. Nightingale's life clearly demonstrates that faith, service, and nursing can and do complement one another in practice. For those who do not share this worldview, the historical influences to nursing are still applicable. It is important to realize that caring and compassion did not derive from a vacuum, but has a definite source and origin.

Lessons from the Good Samaritan

Other internal motivations foundational to nursing practice are empathy and compassion to relieve the suffering of another and meet the other as a fellow human being. Helping people during periods of vulnerability and distress is the essence of what it means to be "good" as a nurse in practice (14). Do we have eyes to see that every patient we care for is our "neighbor" whom we are called to have mercy and compassion on? This timeless truth is situated in the parable of the Good Samaritan taught by Jesus.

A religious leader of the Jews asked Jesus, "Who is my neighbor?" Jesus shared a brief story of a man who was severely beaten, left for dead and was lying on the side of a road. Two religious leaders saw the man, but ignored his plight. But the Samaritan, when he saw the man, demonstrated compassion, dressed his wounds and took him to a place to be cared for. Jesus then asked a question to this religious leader that is relevant to all who provide care for those in need today, *"Which of these three, do you think, proved to be a neighbor to the man who fell among the robbers?"* The religious leader replied, "The one who showed him mercy." Jesus then replied, *"You go, and do likewise"* (Luke 10:29-37).

Influential nurse educator and scholar Patricia Benner validates this truth as relevant to nursing today:

"As nurses, we have been given the ministry and tradition of compassionately caring for strangers, of loving our neighbors as ourselves. We do not have to have great will power to do this, or even great determination and motivation. We do need knowledge and skilled know-how, but we need to be open to see every patient as an opportunity to demonstrate this compassion to those we do not yet know" (15).

Nurse Engagement

Skillful nurse engagement complements caring and compassion and is also foundational to nursing practice and care. It is essential for the nurse to remain clinically curious and responsive to the patient's story and situation. When distracted and not engaged, you will be unable to invest the energy needed to recognize what is currently relevant and urgent that may require intervention. When nurses are not engaged with the patient and their clinical problem, patient outcomes will suffer (14).

You must do your do best to leave personal distractions at the door once you enter the clinical environment. Personal, family and any other stressors or problems will impact the quality of care and nurse engagement needed for practice. Though difficult to fight through at times, recognize the detrimental impact to patient care when you are distracted and unable to focus on the patient you are caring for.

The other side of this coin is the importance of being able to leave work at work. Though certain patients and their situation are not easily forgotten when you leave the practice setting, the challenge that you may experience is the obsessive ruminating over what you could or should have done differently. "Did I forget to do that…" can haunt you at times and even be the source of bad dreams! As long as you did the best you could have done with your knowledge and experience, this is the realistic expectation you must have and the grace you must give yourself as a new nurse.

Spiritual Care

By providing compassionate care, the nurse directly impacts the patient's physical and emotional needs, but holistic care also involves caring for the spirit. But for some of you, spiritual care may conjure up images and expectations of praying with patients and going way out of our comfort zone. Though spiritual care may include prayer it is actually so much more. The essence of spiritual care is caring and serving the whole person: the physical, emotional, social, and spiritual aspects of their being (16). Nurse presence is an essential component to spiritual care as the nurse engages and assesses the "entire" patient with the "entire" nurse (16). It is important to note the distinction between spirituality and religion to promote our understanding of spiritual care.

Spirituality is a broader concept than religion. It represents the innate human beings search for the meaning and purpose in life. Religion is a set of beliefs, texts, and other practices that a community shares in its pursuit of relationship with God or that which is transcendent. Because HOPE and MEANING are key components of spirituality, spiritual care is helping a patient to find/make MEANING out of his/her experience and find HOPE. Practical interventions that we can utilize to facilitate this for a patient include listening, encouraging the expression of feelings, compassionate presence, open-ended questions, instilling hope, and prayer (16).

Though spiritual care is clearly within the nurse's scope of practice, I find that most students as well as nurses in practice are uncomfortable with this responsibility. Contributing factors to this discomfort for some may include the dominant physical/medical model in healthcare, secular-humanistic worldview of educational and healthcare institutions as well as a lack of emphasis on spiritual care in nursing education (87 percent of programs do not have specific content on how to practically incorporate spiritual care in practice!)(16). I have observed that those that are most comfortable with spiritual care find their own faith and spiritual traditions personally meaningful and relevant. When it comes to spirituality you cannot give anything to others if you do not have something within to give. But regardless of where you are in your faith journey, I want to encourage you to embrace this responsibility in some very practical and non-threatening ways so that you can holistically support and care for your patients.

A practical approach to providing holistic spiritual care in your practice is to recapture the perspective that all that you do for your patient can be an act of spiritual care. Instead of compartmentalizing your patient care as "tasks" and spiritual care as something you will do when you have the time, everything you do for your patient (who you view holistically) can become a demonstration of spiritual care. For example, taking a set of vital signs becomes an opportunity for presence and spiritual assessment. You can further intentionalize spiritual care by thinking with every interaction, *"What are this patient's needs, fears, anxieties, or questions?"* Every interaction is filled with meaning as you engage the "entire" patient with yourself wholly engaged (16).

Power of Presence

Did you know that how you use your physical presence while providing care can meet the emotional and even spiritual needs of your patient? To be present means that you are readily AVAILABLE and ACCESSIBLE. This must be done with a spirit that acknowledges your shared humanity with those you care for (5). Presence can also be defined as "being with" and "being there" for the purpose of meeting the needs of your patient in a time of need (17). Presence is when the nurse is centered and focused in the moment of what the patient is currently experiencing. Other categories of presence include caring, nurturance, empathy, physical closeness and physical touch (17). When the nurse is truly present, the nurse is allowed to experience what the patient is feeling (18). Presence is a nursing intervention that can be used in situations where there is nothing more that you can do but BE THERE by being supportive, physically close, offering a touch, or sitting in silence (17). Sitting quietly with your patient in times of need can communicate so much more than any words, even if it is for just a moment.

In contrast a "non-present" nurse would be aloof, outside the situation, or preoccupied with other thoughts though physically present (5). This is the tension you will experience as a new nurse. You will be focused on the "tasks" to be done for your patient, and not "present" in a way that will communicate and demonstrate caring. Give yourself grace to grow and develop as a new nurse, knowing that you will be focused on the tasks that need to be completed, but as you develop a greater proficiency you will soon find yourself having the additional time to be present to your patients.

Presence is also recognized as a nursing intervention by the Nursing Interventions Classifications (NIC). Specific NIC interventions that reflect the use of nurse presence include the following that you can incorporate into your practice:

- Demonstrate accepting attitude.
- Verbally communicate empathy or understanding of the patient's experience.
- Establish patient trust.
- Listen to the patient's concern.
- Touch the patient to express concern as appropriate.

- Remain physically present without expecting interactional responses (19).

In my own practice I have found it helpful to pay close attention to what is in my patient's room. If there is a Bible or other material of a spiritual nature, if/when appropriate, engage the patient regarding their faith and current illness. For example, I recently cared for a patient who had a Bible in his room. I asked, "Do you have a favorite passage, and if so would you like me to read it to you?" He wanted me to read the Twenty-Third Psalm: *"The Lord is my shepherd I shall not want..."* He closed his eyes and was clearly at peace as I read this to him. He thanked me afterwards and asked if I would pray for him. After a short prayer he fell asleep. This took only a couple of minutes, but it clearly ministered and cared for his spirit. I have found that the LITTLE THINGS done at the bedside such as spiritual care are often BIG THINGS to the patient and make a difference to their emotional, spiritual, and even physical well-being.

If you are comfortable with including prayer as part of your care, don't forget that you always have the option to pray FOR your patients. You can do this alone as you provide care, or if you have determined that spirituality is important to your patient, offer to pray for and with them. I have yet to be turned down after thirty years of clinical practice by this request when I have sensed or assessed that this would be meaningful to my patient!

If your patient has definite spiritual concerns or spiritual distress, do not hesitate to contact or make a referral for the chaplain. But the nurse can also implement these spiritual assessment questions to provide support in the present as well as provide documentation in the medical record:

- Are you connected with a faith community? What do you appreciate about this community?
- What is your source of strength, peace, faith, hope, and worth?
- What spiritual practices are important to you?
- How has your health problem affected your spiritual beliefs?
- What can I do to support your faith?
- How do your beliefs help you cope with suffering and illness? (20)

Power of Touch

Another intervention that can minister to the spirit and the heart-felt needs of those you care for is the affection and acceptance that can be communicated by physical touch. The power of physical touch to bring healing and acceptance is powerfully demonstrated in the life and ministry of Jesus. He was approached by a leper who desired healing. In the context of this man's experience, he never experienced the warmth and acceptance of human touch since he became a leper. Instead, he heard daily the loud cries of *"Unclean! Unclean!"* as people moved out of their way to avoid his presence.

Recognizing not only his need to be healed, but also his deep unmet emotional need of acceptance that only human touch could communicate, Jesus reached out and TOUCHED him who was "untouchable" and "unclean."

What can we as caregivers learn from His example? With the increasing prevalence of patients who are in various forms of contact precautions that require the nurse to wear a gown and gloves, what do you think the patient over time feels in this experience? Do they too feel unclean? Recognize the power of touch and be sensitive to the needs of those in contact precautions as well as anyone else whose illness has a similar stigma and is considered "untouchable" or "unclean" by cultural norms today.

Burnout

As you give of yourself as a nurse in practice, there is an inherent possibility of becoming burned-out over time. Any occupation has an inherent risk of burnout, but in nursing how do you know if you are just stressed out or burned out? Burnout is defined as the loss of human caring, or stated another way the separation of caregiving and caring (5). I have experienced burnout firsthand and I hope that you can learn from my experience. When I first started in the ED, it was a dream come true. From the adrenalin rush that came with caring for a critically ill "stab" (short for stabilization or critical) patient, to the wide range of clinical presentations was a stimulating environment for me to be in. I became more proficient in clinical skills and critical thinking as I drew from my prior years of clinical experience. I was engaged and truly cared for what happened to each patient I saw and cared for. I enjoyed what I was doing so much I began to pick up overtime on a regular basis as it was readily available. I was becoming more physically and emotionally tired, but I did not realize that I was beginning to DRIFT.

Slowly but gradually I began not to care. What I once enjoyed, was now just a job and putting in my time. Patients became burdens. I had critical "stabs" and some of these patients died as a result of their injuries or illness. I did not truly care. It was a slow fade, but I knew I had to do something dramatic to recapture my heart. I left the ED and renewed my passion for caring in an entirely different environment in acute care. In addition to a change of scenery, I also needed REST which led to RESToration.

Value of Self-Care

To maintain a healthy balance to prevent burnout in practice you must recognize the value of self-care. This is something that most nurses seem to struggle with. Though this new career path will consume you with new challenges and additional learning, you must not let it become your life! Pursue and fight for the balance that is needed by establishing "margins" in your life. Margins are the blank spaces on a page that we also need in life. Make time for rest, hobbies, relationships, faith, and any other interests that are important to you. If you are a driven Type A like myself, this is easier said than done! I have found the book *Margin: Restoring Emotional, Physical, Financial, and Time Reserves to Overloaded Lives* a needed help in this ongoing battle for balance!

I have seen through my own journey the wisdom of Benner and Wrobel who wrote in *Primacy of Caring*, "It is a peculiarly modern mistake to think that caring is the cause of the burnout and that the cure is to protect oneself from caring to prevent the 'disease' called burnout. Rather, the loss of caring is the sickness, and the return of caring is the recovery" (5, p.473).

There is no reason to remain burned out as a nurse when there are so many opportunities to change the environment you practice in. With the wide variety of acute care units in any hospital, and clinical practice environments in the community, change is readily possible and must be pursued if you ever find yourself drifting in the wrong direction as I did. The ability to further your education and pursue advanced practice roles can ensure that you will remain caring and engaged throughout your career. But introspection and reflection are also needed before making any needed changes. "If I were somewhere else I would be happier" line of thinking may only bring current baggage to a new practice setting and may only be a Band-Aid approach that does not get to the root of contributing factors.

Professionalism in Practice

There is a current crisis of professionalism in nursing today. We are healthcare professionals, but our behavior often betrays this truth with the prevalence of incivility, bullying and disrespectful behavior that is well-documented as a problem in our profession (see appendix A). In one study nurse managers reported an increase in inferior work ethic, poor attendance, and an attitude of entitlement in new nurses entering the profession (21).

What does it mean to be a professional and what does this look like in practice? One study identified the following qualities that defined professionalism in practice; strong interpersonal relationship/communication skills, appearance, time management, being ethical, and having a strong work ethic (21). Practical professionalism is also situated in our American Nurses Association (ANA) Code of Ethics. Section 1.5 Relationships with colleagues and others states the following: "*The principle of **respect** for persons extends to all individuals with whom the nurse interacts. The nurse maintains **compassionate** and **caring** relationships with colleagues and others with a commitment to the fair treatment of individuals, to integrity-preserving compromise, and to resolving conflict*" (22). Professionalism as a nurse can be boiled down to COMPASSION, CARING, and RESPECT. These same core ethics previously addressed in this chapter are also a part of our code of ethics! The same values that we are called to have towards our patients must also be demonstrated to one another.

Practical Professionalism: Reflective Practice

Reflection is a professional behavior that is essential to personal and professional growth as a nurse. If your program had reflective journaling or required you to reflect after each clinical and identify what went well and what could have been improved, you have been well prepared to begin to grow and develop as a new nurse. Reflection is the practice that will make everything you do in the clinical setting a learning opportunity and will strengthen your practice if it is done consistently.

Most of us did not pass skill check-offs the first time. Did you reflect and learn from those mistakes or did you continue to repeat them over and over again? If you graduated from nursing school you obviously did some reflection to identify what went wrong and learned from your error or you would not be reading this book! But in order for reflection to be done well, we must not kick ourselves when we are down and make it personal. "I should never have been a nurse..." I want to break this to you gently, you are human, and you will make mistakes in practice including medication errors. Make every mistake an opportunity for growth and you will actually be the better because of it!

The following summary of professional behaviors are relevant to nursing and have been derived from my own practice as well as those who have been my mentors in nursing. Reflect on each component and make it a priority to internalize and then live out these foundational tenets of professional behavior in practice!

Professionalism is...

1. *Reflective practice.* Reflect on what went well/poorly and make needed adjustments to prevent problems next time. It is also the ability to learn from your mistakes, receive constructive feedback, and grow as a result.
2. *Prompt and prepared.* Be on time and ready to receive report.
3. *Hold yourself to high standards.* Desire to be the best nurse you can be! Be the nurse who you would want, if you needed to be cared for.
4. *Clinically curious.* Ask questions and desire to know the WHY of what you do not know or understand.
5. *Embrace the responsibility.* You are holding the life of another in your hand. Never take this lightly. Take initiative, ownership, and responsibility for the care of your patients, but do not hesitate to ask for help or collaborate with your colleagues as needed!
6. *Caring.* Be truly engaged and empathetic toward those you care for and demonstrate this by your caring presence.
7. *ZERO tolerance for incivility.* Be respectful and direct in all communication.

Additional Resources:

- Book: *Primacy of Caring* by Patricia Benner

- E-Book: *Comfort Theory and Practice A Vision for Holistic Health Care and Research* by Katharine Kolcaba

- Book: *Margin: Restoring Emotional, Physical, Financial, and Time Reserves to Overloaded Lives* by Richard Swenson

Building the "Living" House of Professional Practice

Chapter 2: The Walls: Applied Sciences

Now that our foundation has been established, it is time to build our "living" house! This building has been a work in progress since you started nursing education, but I want to put an exclamation point on content that I have found to be essential to clinical practice. Just like a home that has the walls going up, now we are going to see some tangible progress. But building is also HARD WORK! This is true for any house, but especially the "living" house of professional practice. This hard work is also foundational for you as you enter into practice. This lays the groundwork for the critical and clinical thinking that is required by the nurse discussed in the next chapter. Make it a priority to master the applied sciences of nursing that include pharmacology, anatomy and physiology, and fluids and electrolytes!

Nursing Pharmacology

It has been my experience that comprehension of pharmacology is a struggle for most students. If this is true for you, it is imperative to make this and any content areas that are now a weakness into a strength! You will likely pass medications every day; therefore it is essential to possess a DEEP UNDERSTANDING of pharmacology. Let me share a few principles that I have found helpful and that will lay the brick and mortar for your foundation in clinical practice. In addition to the "rights" of safe medication administration, the following "foundational five" questions must be understood because they relate to essential critical thinking that is needed to safely administer each medication in the clinical setting. These five questions are:

"Foundational Five"

1. What is it for? / What is the pharmacologic class?
2. Why is your patient receiving it?
3. What is the expected patient response based on the mechanism of action?
4. What assessments do you need to know before you administer and then follow up afterward?
5. Is this a safe dose? Is the dose range low-mid-high?

Why the Mechanism of Action Must Be Understood

Anatomy & Physiology is a pre-requisite for most nursing programs and must be integrated into your practice. For example, the classic formula of cardiac output is known to all of you: CO=SVxHR (Cardiac Output=Stroke Volume x Heart Rate). But can you describe how preload, afterload, and contractility influence cardiac output? Do you know how each of these determinates of cardiac output are specifically impacted by the different pharmacologic classifications of cardiac medications? In order to develop a DEEP understanding of the mechanism of action of diuretics, nitrates, beta blockers, calcium channel blockers, and ACE inhibitors, the anatomy and physiology situated in the mechanism of action must be UNDERSTOOD by the nurse to deepen the thinking that is expected by the nurse in professional practice. If this is a weakness for you, you are not alone! I created a handout many years ago that my students have found beneficial to promote and understand this foundational content. It is titled "Comprehending Cardiac Medications" and is found in appendix I.

Clinical practice is like putting a puzzle together. There are many pieces of clinical data and though it may not be readily apparent, most pieces do fit together! In order to put the clinical puzzle together for every patient you will care for, the nurse must be able to recognize clinical relationships. Some of these relationships can be identified in this template of the "foundational five" questions. Is there a clinical relationship between knowing the mechanism of action (#3) and the nursing assessments (#4) you need to know before you give the medication? Absolutely! When the nurse UNDERSTANDS the pathophysiology of the mechanism of action, essential nursing assessments logically follow. Another relationship that must be recognized is the dosage of the medication and acknowledging if the dose range is low, mid, or high. This relationship will suggest the severity of the underlying problem that the medication is treating. The higher the dose range, the more resistive or severe the underlying illness has become.

For example, let's presume you are caring for a patient with hypertension who is receiving atenolol (Tenormin) 75mg po bid. Based on the "foundational five" you would answer these questions in the following way:

1. What is it for? / What is the pharmacologic class?

    HTN/beta blocker

2. Why is your patient receiving it?

    HTN

3. What is the expected patient response based on the mechanism of action?

    Will lower blood pressure because this medication is blocking beta 1 adrenergic receptors on the heart that receive sympathetic nervous system stimulation; therefore the therapeutic effects are decreased BP and heart rate.

4. What assessments do you need to know before you administer and then follow up afterward?
   BP and HR. Hold if SBP <90 or HR <50. Assess for ongoing orthostatic hypotension afterwards.
5. Is this a safe dose? Is the dose range low-mid-high?
   This is a safe dose, IF the patient has ongoing hypertension. This would NOT be a safe dose if this was a new medication or just beginning treatment. This is high range.

By identifying and recognizing these clinical relationships, you understand a beta blocker's mechanism of action, and the most important nursing assessments of documenting the blood pressure and heart rate flow from knowing how this drug physiologically affects the body. Knowing that atenolol (Tenormin) 75mg twice a day is a high dose range, you see the degree of hypertension is likely severe, and may explain why he may be on more than one medication to control his blood pressure.

Informatics & Pharmacology

Though you know many medications well, there are literally thousands of medications you do not know everything needed to administer safely…then what? If you need to administer a medication you are not familiar with and have multiple patients with pressing needs, will you sacrifice safety and wing it? Will you maintain the highest standards of safety even if nobody is watching and determining if you are "safe to give"? To be consistently safe in practice, I strongly recommend that if your institution allows cell phones in the clinical area and you have a smart phone or can purchase an iPod Touch, make an investment in a nursing drug reference manual that you will carry with you at all times in the clinical setting. Your institution may provide pharmacology software that can assist you with your assessment of dosages and compatibility. If so, please take the time to look up the medication you are questioning. One minute of research may save you hours later in paperwork and the courtroom.

This is a relevant application of the QSEN competency of informatics. Informatics is defined as the ability of the nurse to "use information and technology to communicate, manage knowledge, mitigate error, and support decision making" (1). In order to effectively use technology the nurse must also value the ability of tech-based resources to support clinical decision making and its ability to help prevent errors in practice (1).

My personal favorite application of informatics technology is *Davis's Drug Guide for Nurses*. Trust me, it is well worth the current $49.95 download for a number of reasons. It can be stored on your device's memory so it does not have to be on or connected to the internet. Having this resource is the equivalent of having over 5,000 medication cards at your disposal in seconds!

If you want to have additional resources on your mobile device in addition to a drug guide, Skyscape has an excellent selection of more than 200 nursing specific downloads so you can build your own nursing informatics library! I have found the Skyscape platform to be the easiest to navigate. It is recommended to have all of your electronic resources on the same platform. This is another advantage to using Skyscape. I have found *Davis's Comprehensive Handbook of Laboratory and Diagnostic Tests with Nursing Implications* an excellent companion to a drug guide to promote and build your knowledge of lab values. Having quick accessibility while at the patient's chart is PRICELESS!

Diseases and Disorders: A Nursing Therapeutics Manual will help develop needed critical thinking by understanding the pathophysiology of your patient's primary problem. An additional benefit to having these three resources on your electronic device is the ability to develop the foundational nurse thinking skill of identifying CLINICAL RELATIONSHIPS. Skyscape has the ability to SmartLink,™ which is a tool that enables you to cross-reference all of your Skyscape resources, quickly and easily. Let's assume you have these three resources discussed above on your electronic device. You access the topic of heart failure on *Diseases and Disorders.* When you SmartLink,™ the drugs that are used to manage heart failure and the laboratory values specific to heart failure are identified and can be easily accessed on the other resources. This will promote your learning and facilitate putting the clinical puzzle together.

This is a summary of the reasons that these resources should be included in your practice:
1. Accessibility
    a. When you need medication or other clinical information fast, do you have time to retrieve and look it up in a hard copy nursing drug or lab manual? This can take minutes compared to seconds with a touch screen.
    b. Using free online resources through your employer, such as Micromedex, may be an option, but I have found it to be "TMI" (Too Much Information) and content heavy as it is geared for physicians and pharmacists, while a nursing drug guide is concise and "just right."
    c. You can purchase a belt clip holster to carry your smart phone or iPod Touch with you at all times (if your institution allows).

2. Nursing emphasis vs. physician emphasis
    a. Though Micromedex or Epocrates are free downloads for your smart phone, they are geared for physician practice and do not have essential content that nurses require. Though you can get the basics of drug action, side effects, dosages, etc. from these free

resources, if you have to give an IV push of metoprolol (Lopressor) 5 mg (or any IV drug), how quickly can you administer it, and what is the onset-peak-duration of this drug or any drug you administer? Do you need to monitor the patient's blood pressure during administration? You will rarely find it in Micromedex or Epocrates; therefore a nursing drug reference is essential to safe practice.

   b. If you want to get started with a drug reference guide at no cost, I have found that that the abbreviated content found in the application Micromedex is more relevant and richer in detail than Epocrates. Under the "Administration" tab of Micromedex, some of the IV med push times are identified, but not consistently.

3. Usage
   a. Would you come to clinical without your stethoscope? Accessible nursing references are just as essential. Even though I have been an RN for thirty years, I do not leave home without my Davis's Drug and Davis's Labs on my smart phone!

Need-to-Know Medications

One of your objectives as a new nurse is to build on your knowledge of medications so you are less and less reliant on a nursing drug reference manual. With over 5,000 medications used in practice, which medications are most commonly used and relevant? This will vary based on your practice setting and geographic location. Based on my clinical experience in acute care in the Midwest, I have created a handout titled **"Most Commonly Used Categories of Medications"** found in appendix H, which identifies the most commonly used categories of medications, individual medications in that category, most common side effects, and essential nursing interventions. I have also created a short list of forty-five of the most commonly used individual medications that are used most often in acute care. I encourage you to make your own list based on your practice area as well. Once this list is mastered, it will lay a strong foundation of pharmacology to your practice!

Start with mastering each of these forty-five medications by being able to answer the "foundational five" questions. In order to promote your learning I have included a blank medication sheet that can be reproduced and can be found in appendix D. You can personalize this list based on your needs and most commonly administered medications. I encourage you to complete this worksheet for those medications you do not know. This will also prepare you for the NCLEX if you have not yet taken it. Your goal is to answer from memory each of these "foundational five" questions for the medications below:

1. What is it for? / What is the pharmacologic class?
2. Why is your patient receiving it?

3. What is the expected patient response based on the mechanism of action?
4. What assessments do you need to know before you administer and then follow up afterward?
5. Is this a safe dose? Is the dose range low-mid-high?

Most Common Medications That Must Be Mastered (Generic names)

Anti-hypertensives B-blockers: Atenolol/Metoprolol ACE-I: Captopril/Lisinopril Ca+-channel blockers: Diltiazem **Anti-arrhythmic** Amiodarone Digoxin **Diuretics** Loop: Furosemide Thiazide: HCTZ K+ sparing: Spironolactone **Lipid lowering** Statins (all) **Anti-coagulants** Warfarin Heparin/Enoxaparin	**Respiratory** Albuterol fluticasone/salmeterol (Advair Diskus) **GI** H2 blocker: Ranitidine/Famotidine PPI-Pantoprazole/Omeprazole Ondansetron/Metoclopramide Docusate/Senna **Diabetic** All insulin's Humalog/Novolog Regular/NPH Lente Glyburide/Metformin **Misc.** Potassium chloride Levothyroxine Prednisone/Methylprednisolone	**Non-opioid Analgesics** Ketorolac Acetaminophen Ibuprofen **Opioid Analgesics** Hydromorphone Morphine Percocet/Vicodin (trade name) **Anti-anxiety** Lorazepam/Diazepam **Anti-Infectives** Ciprofloxacin Vancomycin Metronidazole Cefazolin piperacillin/tazobactam (Zosyn)

Understanding Labs: Why Fluids & Electrolytes Must Be Mastered!

In addition to pharmacology, another consistent struggle some nursing students exhibit has been related to fluids and electrolytes (F&E). F&E is seen as another dreaded topic to endure and pass. Though this content is difficult and requires application of chemistry, acid/base, and physiology, it is relevant and foundational to practice and must not only be understood but MASTERED by the new nurse. Laboratory values provide an early window to physiologic status changes that may not be evident in vital signs or assessment data collected by the nurse. Examples seen in clinical practice are TRENDS of an elevated serum lactate in any shock state, including septic, elevated neutrophils, bands, or WBC that are often seen in sepsis, or elevated serum creatinine in acute renal failure or severe dehydration. Early identification of sepsis can save lives. A low blood pressure, elevated heart rate, and elevated serum lactate would cue the nurse that this patient is becoming septic.

Because of the sheer amount of data (TMI!) in routine laboratory panels, these are difficult to sort through and the new nurse has difficulty identifying which values are most relevant to the primary problem. I have two resources that my students have found beneficial to promote their learning. One is a handout titled "Clinical Lab Values and Nursing Responsibilities" and is found in appendix G. The other resource is the clinical reasoning case studies that you can work through after reading this book. (Sepsis Unfolding Clinical Reasoning Case Study is included in chapter 5). Each case study begins with a clinical scenario and contains numerous labs that must be recognized as clinically significant to the nurse. Once you have completed the clinical reasoning questions from the student version of the case study, you will compare your answers with a thoroughly developed faculty key that goes into great depth and detail regarding the rationale for the labs that must be recognized as clinically relevant and why. This will promote your learning and mastery because this content is contextualized to clinical practice at the bedside.

Lab Planning

A practical nurse thinking skill that I emphasized with my students in the clinical setting was the ability of the nurse to develop a plan of care based on relevant abnormal labs on their patient. I call this "LAB PLANNING" and will show you how this works. For example, if you have a patient who has been admitted for heart failure exacerbation and his creatinine has increased from a baseline of 1.4 and is now 2.5, and the B-Natriuretic Peptide (BNP) has increased from a baseline of 180 and is now 1255, the nurse can use these relevant abnormal findings to create a "lab plan of care" that will dovetail with traditional nursing care priorities based on his primary problem. Because creatinine is a key indicator of renal function and perfusion and the BNP represents the degree of ventricular stretch and overload, the nurse must recognize the need to include these "lab planning" nursing interventions:

Lab Plan of Care

Relevant Lab:	Nursing Interventions:
Creatinine: 2.5 (0.6-1.2 mg/dL)	1. Assess urine output and I&O. Determine if minimum of 30 mL/hour of urine output is present 2. Fluid restriction if ordered 3. Assess for signs of fluid retention/edema 4. Assess daily weight and trend daily 5. Assess Glomerular Filtration Rate (GFR)

Relevant Lab:	Nursing Interventions:
BNP: 1255 (<100)	1. Assess respiratory status for tachypnea and breath sounds for basilar or scattered crackles (may be fine or course crackles depending on severity) 2. Assess HR and SBP carefully to promote decreased cardiac workload

	(heart rate <80 and SBP <140
	3. Assess tolerance to activity
	4. Assess I&O and urine output
	5. Assess lower extremities for any pitting edema present

As a clinical adjunct faculty, I quickly realized that many students struggled with this important concept so I created a handout students could use to situate the most common lab values that are relevant to practice and the essential nursing assessments and interventions to create their own "lab plan" with their patient. This handout is found in appendix G and is titled "Clinical Lab Values and Nursing Responsibilities."

In addition to recognizing the most relevant labs for your patient and their primary problem to create a "lab plan of care," there are also lab values that are ALWAYS relevant if they are ordered and present because of their physiologic importance and relevance to homeostasis and well-being. If present in the chart, the following labs must be noted and TRENDED! Normal ranges are listed for each lab. I have selected these ALWAYS relevant labs based on my own observations in clinical practice:

ALWAYS Relevant Labs

Lab	Relevance/Rationale
Sodium (Na+) 135-145 mEq/L	I consider Na+ the "Crystal-Light" electrolyte. Though this is simplistic, it does help to understand in principle how foundational Na+ is to fluid balance. When you add one small packet of Crystal Light to your 16 ounce bottle of water, the concentration is just right. This is where a normal Na+ will be (135-145). Where free water goes, sodium will follow to a degree. Therefore if there is a fluid volume deficit due to dehydration, Na+ will typically be elevated due to being concentrated (less water). If there is fluid volume excess Na+ will be diluted and will likely be low. It is the "foundational" fluid balance electrolyte!
Potassium (K+) 3.5-5.0 mEq/L	Essential to normal cardiac electrical conduction as is Mg+. If too high or low can predispose to rhythm changes that can be life threatening! K+ tends to deplete more quickly with loop diuretic usage than Mg+. K+ and Mg+ are essential cardiac electrolytes and are therefore ALWAYS relevant!
Magnesium (Mg+) 1.6-2.0 mEq/L	Essential to normal cardiac electrical conduction as is K+. If too high or low can predispose to rhythm changes that can be life threatening! K+ and Mg+ are essential cardiac electrolytes and are therefore ALWAYS relevant! Skeletal muscle if too low, patients will have beats of clonus with deep tendon reflexes.
Creatinine 0.6-1.2 mg/dL or Glomerular Filtration	GOLD STANDARD for kidney function and adequacy of renal perfusion; therefore it is ALWAYS relevant!

Rate (GFR) >60 mL/minute	
Hemoglobin Male: 13.5-17.5 g/dL Female: 12.0-16.0	GOLD STANDARD to determine anemia or acute/chronic blood loss.
WBC 4500-11,000/mm 3	ALWAYS RELEVANT based on its correlation to the presence of inflammation or infection. Will usually be increased if infection present.
Neutrophils 50-70%	ALWAYS RELEVANT for same reason as WBC's. Are the most common leukocyte and their role as a FIRST RESPONDER to any bacterial infection within several hours must be noted. The more aggressive or systemic the infection, the higher the percentage of neutrophils and WBC's. Bands greater than 8 are also clinically significant and must be clustered with WBC and neutrophils to determine if sepsis is a clinical concern.

In the most common lab panels that are ordered, the remaining labs listed below must also be understood because of their physiologic significance. Depending on the primary problem of your patient, these labs may be relevant, but it depends! The normal ranges are listed for each lab, but note that depending on how each lab calculates values, these ranges can vary slightly between institutions so validate what is normal for your institution!

Basic Metabolic Panel (BMP)

Chloride (95-105 mEq/L)
- Relevant if NG suction or frequent vomiting is present due to loss of hydrochloric HCl acid. Chloride is the Cl- of hydrochloric acid.

CO_2 (22-28 mEq/L)
- Relevant when there are acid-base concerns. Though it is CO_2 on a BMP and you are thinking carbon dioxide, it is actually reflecting the amount of HCO_3-!

Anion Gap (AG) (7-16 mEq/l)
- This is the difference between primary measured cations ($Na+$ and $K+$) and the primary measured anions (chloride $Cl-$ and bicarbonate HCO_3-) in serum. Useful with acid/base concerns typically seen in renal failure.

Glucose (Fasting: 70-110 mg/dL)
- Relevant with history of diabetes. Elevated levels post op increase risk of infection/sepsis.

Calcium (8.4-10.2 mg/dL)
- Relevant with renal failure, ETOH abuse. Low albumin can cause hypocalcemia, while elevated levels can be seen with cancer (with and without bone metastases).

BUN (7 - 25 mg/dl)
- I use creatinine as most relevant/important lab to determine renal function. I do not consistently use BUN in practice as it can be elevated for other reasons rather that renal, though it is relevant with renal failure to trend with creatinine.

Miscellaneous Chemistries

Lactate (0.5-2.2 mmol/L)
- Not routinely done, but when present in chart it is there for a reason! Remember Krebs cycle and lactic acidosis in A&P due to anaerobic metabolism? GOLD STANDARD lab to trend with any shock state especially sepsis! Elevated levels correlate with higher likelihood of dying. For example, in septic shock a level >4 reflects a 28% mortality. Lactate builds up within the serum and can be seen as a marker of strained cellular metabolism.

Phosphorus (2.5-4.5 mg/dl)
- 85% stored in bones. Primary intracellular anion and responsible for cellular metabolism and formation of bones and teeth. Relevant in renal failure and will be increased due to decreased renal excretion.

Ionized Calcium (1.05-1.46 mmol/L)
- Represents Ca++ that is metabolically available compared to serum Ca++ that is more generalized. This value is more accurate determinate of calcium and if low, serum calcium is usually also decreased.

Amylase (25-125 U/l)
- Digestive enzyme to break down complex carbohydrates. Primarily formed in pancreas and will "leak" into circulation with pancreatic inflammation.
- Relevant with pancreatitis/cholecystitis and obstruction of common bile duct that leads to pancreatic inflammation.

Lipase (3-73 units/L)
- Glycoprotein produced primarily in pancreas to break down fats. Will "leak" into circulation with pancreatic inflammation. Relevant with pancreatitis/cholecystitis and obstruction of common bile duct that leads to pancreatic inflammation.

Complete Blood Count

Hematocrit (male: 39-49% female: 35-45%)
- In comparison to hemoglobin is not as relevant though elevation can be seen to confirm fluid volume deficit–will be concentrated and elevated in this context.

RBC's (male: 4.3-5.7 (x108/µl) female: 3.8-5.1 (x108/ µl)
- Identifies the number of RBC's in a cubic millimeter. In anemia or when there has been a significant blood loss, hemoglobin is the GOLD STANDARD that must be noted. I rarely find this value relevant as most practitioners emphasize the hemoglobin in practice.

Platelet count (150-450 x 103/μl)
- Relevant whenever there is a concern for anemia or blood loss or on heparin. If this is low it will obviously be significant and must be noted. Any patient on heparin products must also have this noted because of the clinical possibility of heparin induced thrombocytopenia (HIT), which is when the immune system forms antibodies against heparin that causes small clots and therefore lowers platelet levels.

WBC Differential

Band forms (3-5%)
- Immature neutrophils that are elevated in sepsis as the body attempts to fight infection and releases these prematurely. If elevated is a clinical RED FLAG in the context of sepsis. If elevated to 8, then is considered a "shift to the left" which means impending sepsis.

Lymphocytes (23-33%)
- Relevant when there is a known or suspected VIRAL infection.

Monocytes (3-7%)
- Are phagocytes similar to neutrophils, but not as dominant, nor are they as clinically significant and relevant to practice as neutrophils.

Eosinophils (1-3%)
- Elevated with parasitic infections or allergic responses.

Basophils (0-1%)
- Are phagocytes but not as dominant, nor are they as clinically significant and relevant to practice as neutrophils.

Liver Panel
(Relevance in this panel will depend on the primary problem and chief complaint, but if patient has Gastro intestinal (GI) primary problem then they are ALL relevant!

Albumin (3.5-5.5 g/dL)
- Is a large colloid plasma protein made by the liver. Because it is a protein it will be decreased in malnutrition. Therefore it can be a contributing factor to ascites or edema.

Total Bilirubin (0.1-1.0 mg/dL // 0.0-0.3 mg/dL)
- Total of both direct/indirect bilirubin. Bilirubin is metabolized by the liver and broken down by-product of heme protein in RBC's. Relevant in any liver disease.

Alkaline Phosphatase (male: 38-126 U/l female: 70-230 U/l)
- Nonspecific hepatic isoenzyme that has large concentration in liver, but found in other parts of the body. If there is a primary liver disease focus on ALT, AST as these are much more specific to liver function.

ALT (8-20 U/L)
- Relevant with any primary liver disease. Enzyme found in liver. Is released into circulation when liver cells are damaged.

AST (8-20 U/L)
- Relevant with any primary liver disease. Enzyme found in liver. Is released into circulation when liver cells are damaged.

Urinalysis

Color (yellow)
- Make this part of your practice to intentionally assess directly as well as if in a UA. Clear to pale yellow is usually seen with aggressive diuresis. Orange color typically due to bilirubin in urine with liver disease. Dark amber is commonly seen with dehydration or fluid volume deficit.

Clarity (clear)
- Though the context here is a UA, recognize the importance of always evaluating the clarity in the tubing of any patient with a Foley catheter. If urine is cloudy or has sediment reflects possible UTI and UA should be obtained, especially if new finding.

Specific Gravity (1.015-1.030)
- Measures the kidney's ability to concentrate or dilute urine in relation to plasma. Increased with dehydration and decreased with diuresis.

Protein (neg)
- Relevant when positive in any patient with renal disease. If kidneys have been damaged or new finding of renal failure, proteins being a large colloid should be filtered by glomerulus. If there is damage to the glomeruli, the inability to adequately filter urine will be present and therefore will be positive. However, in active young adolescent females there is a phenomenon that produces a higher protein in the urine. A first voiding of the day should be measured with these individuals.

Glucose (neg)
- Relevant if diabetic–degree of presence in urine reflects poorly controlled the diabetes. Also same rationale as protein above. Glucose is also a large particle that should be filtered by glomerulus.

Ketones (neg)
- Ketones are formed from metabolism of fatty acids. Relevant and most commonly seen in DKA and dehydration.

Bilirubin (neg)
- Must be noted and relevant with liver disease. Should be negative, but with liver disease may be positive.

Blood (neg)
- Will be positive if has UTI or renal calculi.

Nitrite (neg)
- To rule out UTI or determine if present, nitrites, LET, and WBC micro must be assessed together. Nitrites are relevant because if positive, reflect the presence of gram negative bacteria in the urinary tract, the most common being E. coli. By itself is not a predictable indicator of urinary infection.

LET (Leukocyte Esterase) (neg)
- To rule out UTI or determine if present, nitrites, LET, and WBC micro must be assessed together. LET is relevant–is an enzyme that is present if WBC's are in the urine. By itself is not a predictable indicator of urinary infection.

UA Micro

RBC's (<5)
- Must be noted if UTI or renal calculi–this gives amount of RBC's present which can correlate with severity.

WBC's (<5)
- ALWAYS RELEVANT & GOLD STANDARD that by itself indicates the presence of UTI if has symptoms. Most clinicians will diagnose UTI if >5 WBC's present in urine and symptomatic. Amount of WBC's present indicates severity. To rule out UTI or determine if present, nitrites, LET, and WBC micro must be assessed together.

Bacteria (neg)
- Does not consistently correlate to presence of infection, though it can be clustered with WBC, LET, and nitrites.

Epithelial (neg)
- Skin cells that are present but not relevant in itself.

Cardiac

Troponin (<0.4 ng/mL)
- When ordered to rule out myocardial infarction, it is ALWAYS RELEVANT as it is the most sensitive cardiac marker that will be elevated if there is cardiac muscle damage. Can take up to 6 hours after chest pain to elevate so are always ordered every 6-8 hours x3 and each is carefully trended to the prior to see if trend is increasing and positive.

- Is very sensitive cardiac marker that can be slightly elevated and positive in heart failure and unstable angina.

- Those with renal disease, usually CKD III-IV, will be unable to clear troponin by the kidneys and may have a baseline that is a low level positive. This is why it is so important to TREND the current level to the most recent in chart and determine if there is a clinical concern in this context.

CPK total (Male: 38-174 U/l Female: 26-140 U/l)
- Enzyme that is found in muscle fibers of the body. Is not generalized to cardiac muscle. CPK is used as a ratio to MB to identify if the ratio of CPK to CPK-MB is clinically significant and positive for a MI.

CPK-MB (<5%)
- Specific iso-enzyme for cardiac muscle. If this is elevated, confirms presence of MI. Because troponin can be sensitive, many physicians order both troponin and CPK-MB to correlate. If troponins slightly positive but CPK-MB negative, most physicians would not diagnose an MI.

BNP (B-natriuretic Peptide) (<100 ng/L)
- What troponins are to MI, BNP is to heart failure. It is a neurohormone secreted by myocytes in the ventricles. When ventricles are stressed and overloaded, BNP is a compensatory hormone that is a vasodilator and also diuretic to help the body naturally decrease the workload of the heart. It will be elevated in heart failure exacerbation.

Coagulation

PT/INR (0.9-1.1 nmol/L)
- Measures time required for a firm fibrin clot to form and measures the clotting cascade. Is dependent on vitamin K synthesis from the liver. Therefore will be elevated in liver disease without being on warfarin. Standard coag. ordered for those on warfarin (Coumadin) to maintain therapeutic goal of INR 2-3.

- Relevant and must be noted for any patient on warfarin but especially when a bleeding complication secondary to warfarin presents. Warfarin can be reversed quickly if active bleeding through administering vitamin K IV and or fresh frozen plasma. (2)

Trending to Rescue

Trending ALL RELEVANT clinical data is foundational to thinking like a nurse and incorporating clinical reasoning in practice. It is this consistent trending and comparison of all relevant clinical data that will allow the nurse to identify and capture trends that may reflect a concerning change in patient status. Recognizing there is a problem through vigilant trending will allow the nurse to rescue their patient and initiate needed nursing interventions before an adverse outcome becomes apparent.

In order to do this when you care for each of your patients you must be able to identify what lab values and assessments are the most RELEVANT based on the PRIMARY PROBLEM. This is the transfer of knowledge from the classroom to the bedside that is required and expected of the nurse. The clinical reasoning case studies you will work through are invaluable because they will allow you to PRACTICE this foundational skill of trending to rescue through realistic clinical scenarios that unfold slowly, just like in clinical practice. They will require you to identify what clinical data is RELEVANT, and what must be recognized as clinically significant to the nurse.

For every patient you care for, you must carefully note and TREND the following clinical data (if it is present depending on your clinical setting) from the chart as well as nurse to nurse report and then once again when you personally assess your patient for the first time:

ALWAYS RELEVANT Laboratory Values
(if present in chart)
- Chemistries
  - Potassium
  - Sodium
  - Magnesium
  - Creatinine/GFR
- CBC
  - WBC
  - Neutrophils
  - Hgb.
  - Platelets
- Cardiac
  - CPK-MB
  - Troponin
  - BNP
- Coags
  - INR/PT

- UA
  - WBC-micro
  - Gram stain
  - LET
  - Nitrates

Nurse Collected Data that must be TRENDED

Vital Signs
- Temperature
- Heart rate
- Respiratory rate
- Blood pressure
- O2 saturation
- Pain

Nursing Assessment
Respiratory
- Breath sounds
- Rhythm/character
- O2 amount/delivery (if applicable)

Cardiac
- Heart sounds
- Strength/regularity of peripheral pulses
- Cap refill
- Color/temperature extremities
- Telemetry rhythm (if applicable)
- Edema—location/amount/pitting vs. non-pitting
- Breath sounds
- Rhythm/character
- O2 amount/delivery (if applicable)

Neuro
- a/o x4 (person-place-time-situation)
- Level of consciousness (LOC)
- Movement/sensation in extremities

GI
- Appearance of abdomen
- Tenderness w/palpation
- Bowel sounds/flatus/LBM (last bowel movement)

GU
- Urine amount/color/clarity
- Foley—secured/urethral drainage?

Skin
- Color/temperature
- Skin integrity—redness/blanchable over pressure points if present?

Psychosocial
- Emotional support/needs
- Spiritual care/needs
- Educational priorities

I&O
- Shift and 24 hour trends if relevant
- Daily weights. Remember that for every 1 kg. of weight loss/gain this represents 1000 mL of volume.

Additional Resources:

If you are a visual learner, the first six resources are by the same primary author and are unique in that they utilize cartoon style illustrations and pneumonics to promote student learning of the applied sciences of nursing discussed in this chapter.

- Book: *Memory Notebook of Nursing Vol. 1* by Joann Graham Zerwekh, Jo Carol Claborn & C.J. Miller

- Book: *Memory Notebook of Nursing: A Collection of Visual Images and Memonics to Increase Memory and Learning, Vol. 2* by Joann Graham Zerwekh, Jo Carol Claborn & C.J. Miller

- Book: *Memory Notebook of Nursing: Pharmacology & Diagnostics* by Joann Graham Zerwekh, Jo Carol Claborn & C.J. Miller

- Flashcards: *Mosby's Pharmacology Memory NoteCards: Visual, Mnemonic, and Memory Aids for Nurses, 3rd ed.* by Joann Graham Zerwekh, Jo Carol Claborn & Tom Gaglione

- Flashcards: *Mosby's Fluids & Electrolytes Memory NoteCards: Visual, Mnemonic, and Memory Aids for Nurses, 2nd ed.* by Joann Graham Zerwekh, Jo Carol Claborn & Tom Gaglione

- Flashcards: *Mosby's Pathophysiology Memory NoteCards: Visual, Mnemonic, and Memory Aids for Nurses, 2nd ed.* by Joann Graham Zerwekh, Jo Carol Claborn & Tom Gaglione

- Flashcards: *Maxi Learn* (a pre-structured drug card system)

- FREE Download: *Drug Card Template* (Maxi Learn) http://site.maxi-learn.org/uploads/Maxi_Learn_Drug_Card_Template.pdf

Building the "Living" House of Professional Practice

Chapter 3: The Roof: Thinking like a Nurse

You have worked hard to build the walls of your "living" house of professional practice but now the real work has just begun! It is time for the heavy lifting of getting the roof trusses in place that will tie all four walls of your house together and give them strength. The "roof" of THINKING LIKE A NURSE is the weakest link for most new nurses for a number of reasons. Lack of clinical experience limits your ability to build on prior experiences to promote your learning and nurse thinking in practice. A foundational "nurse thinking" skill that prepares the nurse to critically and clinically think and reason is the ability to identify CLINICAL RELATIONSHIPS. When these relationships are recognized, most of the information collected by the nurse begins to "fit" and the clinical puzzle begins to come together. Before we discuss the higher level of thinking that is needed by the nurse in clinical practice, let's take a closer look at recognizing and identifying clinical relationships.

Recognizing Clinical Relationships

In practice there is no shortage of clinical data that must be sorted and filtered by the nurse to determine if it is relevant to the care of your patient. It is important to recognize that most of the clinical data in the chart as well as what you collect at the bedside has a relationship to the other. Once these clinical relationships are recognized, you will be able to put the pieces of the clinical puzzle together. The identification of the significance of relevant data is the foundation for you to make correct clinical judgments that will form the foundation for clinical reasoning as you care for your patients.

In order to identify how clinical data is related and its relevance to the primary problem, there are a series of questions you can ask yourself to help determine if a clinical relationship is present. These are the most common clinical relationships that I use in my own practice to help put the clinical puzzle together for every patient I care for:

Clinical Relationships that Must Be Recognized by the Nurse
1. *Identify the RELATIONSHIP of what current medications are treating past medical problems.*
2. *Is there a RELATIONSHIP between any problem in their past medical history that contributed to the development of the current primary problem?*
3. *What is the RELATIONSHIP between the primary problem and the current chief complaint?*

4. *What is the RELATIONSHIP between relevant clinical data and the primary problem?*
5. *What is the RELATIONSHIP between newly ordered medications and the primary problem?*

By reflecting on these five questions and then utilizing the template of clinical reasoning questions, you will be well on your way to THINKING LIKE A NURSE in practice! These five clinical relationships are further defined and explained below.

1. ***Identify the RELATIONSHIP of what current medications are treating past medical problems.***

If your patient is receiving atenolol (Tenormin) they most likely have a history of hypertension. To identify this clinical relationship the nurse must know not only what the medication is for, but based on their patient's history why are they receiving it. If there is no documented history of hypertension but they have a history of atrial fibrillation, is there a relationship between atrial fibrillation and atenolol? Absolutely! If you understand the mechanism of action of a beta blocker, you can situate your knowledge of atrial fibrillation to recognize that they often have rapid ventricular response or HR>100. Once this relationship is recognized, the pieces of the clinical puzzle begin to come together because this medication is given to prevent or keep the heart rate within normal limits. If you can identify these clinical relationships you are well on your way to thinking like a nurse in clinical practice!

2. ***Is there a RELATIONSHIP between any problem in their past medical history that contributed to the development of the current primary problem?***

I call this the DOMINO effect and if you have a basic understanding of pathophysiology, you can see that when one domino (problem) begins to fall it affects the next domino and causes another problem to develop as a consequence. If your patient has a history of hypertension, hyperlipidemia, MI, ischemic cardiomyopathy, and has an ejection fraction of 20 percent, is there a relationship between any of these problems? Absolutely! Each of these illnesses was influenced by the other. To take this question to the next level, put these illnesses that are related to one another in the chronological order they likely occurred in this patient.

This is the order that is most likely: hyperlipidemia as well as hypertension is going to cause underlying damage to the arterial vessels that will accelerate the development of atherosclerosis. This will then cause the next domino to fall which is an acute MI. Because of chronic ischemia secondary to progressive atherosclerosis and the MI, the ischemic cardiomyopathy domino has now fallen. Finally, as the cardiomyopathy progresses, the ejection fraction domino falls and is reflected by a deterioration of function from a normal range of 60-65%, to now only 20%.

3. What is the RELATIONSHIP between the primary problem and the current chief complaint?

If we use the same patient that we situated above who is now admitted with an exacerbation of heart failure, whose chief complaint was SOB, decreased tolerance to activity, and weight gain of five pounds in the last two days, you should be able to see the RELATIONSHIP between these symptoms and heart failure exacerbation. But if I were to ask you WHY the patient developed these symptoms due to exacerbation of heart failure, in other words state the concise pathophysiology of left-sided heart failure and how it has progressed to right-sided failure, could you do this readily?

This is your goal in clinical practice, which must also be done to understand the rationale for physician orders as well as nursing interventions to manage this patient's care. If you have a patient whose primary medical problem you do not know or have not seen before, make it a priority to go to a medical/physician database to understand the pathophysiology and rationale for all that is done. My favorite web-based database that is geared to physicians and other healthcare professionals to understand the pathophysiology and related clinical data with almost any problem is www.emedicine.com.

4. What is the RELATIONSHIP between relevant clinical data and the primary problem?

Let's continue with our example of a patient with heart failure. Clinical data includes physical assessment findings, vital signs, and laboratory values. Your relevant assessment findings with our patient in heart failure reveal 2+ pitting edema in lower legs, and coarse crackles half up bilaterally. The respiratory rate is 24/minute with O2 sats 88 percent on room air and BP is 178/88. The creatinine has increased from 1.1 to current values of 1.9 and BNP is 1125. Though you may know that this data reflects heart failure exacerbation, the goal in clinical practice is to understand the relationship and pathophysiology of this data to the primary problem.

Based on this clinical data, what data supports right-sided heart failure, and what data reflects left-sided heart failure? (2+ pitting edema is right-sided failure, while the crackles reflect left). Is there a relationship between left-sided failure, crackles, RR 24, and O2 sats 88 percent? Is the blood pressure too high? What is the significance of this finding in this patient? Finally, the laboratory values must be understood and situated with the primary medical problem. Why would the creatinine be elevated? If you can recognize the relationship between decreased cardiac output from heart failure exacerbation and kidney perfusion, you are on your way to thinking like a nurse! The BNP is also elevated. The relationship of left ventricular stress and overload and this neurohormone must be recognized. In addition to recognizing that the BNP is elevated in heart failure exacerbation, could you state what physiologic effect BNP has on the body? This too must be understood. The body was designed with a number of compensatory mechanisms and BNP acts as a vasodilator and has diuretic effects that lower preload as well as afterload and the workload of the heart when in heart failure.

5. *What is the RELATIONSHIP between newly ordered medications and the primary problem?*

If this same patient with heart failure exacerbation has new orders of furosemide (Lasix) 40 mg IV push and nitroglycerin IV gtt-titrate to keep SBP <140, it is important to understand the rationale for the primary care provider's orders and plan of care as well as your own as a nurse. This is when your knowledge of the mechanism of action of each of these medications will make this relationship clear. Furosemide (Lasix) is a loop diuretic that will promote potent diuresis and, therefore, remove excess fluid and decrease preload. Why would the primary care provider want the SBP <140 and how will nitroglycerin IV drip accomplish this stated objective? Does an elevated SBP and increased afterload increase the workload of the heart? Is this going to help or hurt this patient with heart failure? Knowing that nitroglycerin dilates coronary arteries for those with angina, but also dilates systemic venous circulation, will benefit this patient by decreasing preload as well as afterload. This will also decrease the workload of the heart, our primary objective with exacerbation of heart failure.

It is also important for the nurse to recognize how the mechanism of action of the drugs ordered can initiate a "domino" cascade that must also be understood. Many heart failure patients are on beta-blockers. How does this drug affect cardiac contractility? Could this be a problem with our patient in heart failure? Absolutely! It is not uncommon for physicians to lower afterload through the use of beta-blockers such as atenolol (Tenormin). In addition to lowering heart rate and blood pressure, they also decrease cardiac contractility. Therefore, the effect of beta-blockers can also cause a "domino" of heart failure exacerbation and the symptoms commonly seen such as increased edema and shortness of breath.

If this was not readily known to you, make this emphasis of understanding the relationships of clinical data a priority so you can deepen your ability to clinically reason and think like a nurse in practice!

Clinical Reasoning=Nurse Thinking

What will your nursing priorities be when the status of your patient suddenly changes? If your program taught NANDA nursing diagnostic statements as the ONLY way to establish nursing priorities, this reliance on NANDA nursing diagnostic statements may be a barrier to properly prioritize if there is a change in status (1). In order to provide safe, accurate, and effective care, it is essential for you to THINK IN ACTION and be able to transfer learning from the classroom to the bedside. The nurse is a knowledge worker who uses information and must be able to translate this knowledge into action to deliver safe patient care (2). Nursing practice requires correct judgments and appropriate responses to life-threatening conditions. Just as a lifeguard must be able to recognize that there is a struggling person in the water who is in need of rescue in order to save their life, the nurse must also be able to recognize a patient who has SUBTLE changes that are also in need of "rescue." I have seen firsthand in clinical practice that when a nurse fails to recognize relevant trends, situate their knowledge, and clinically reason, patients will experience an adverse outcome and may even die as a result.

In order to THINK LIKE A NURSE you must understand and then incorporate CLINICAL REASONING into your practice. Clinical reasoning is the ability of the nurse to THINK IN ACTION and REASON as a situation CHANGES over time by capturing and understanding the significance of clinical trajectories and grasping the essence of the current clinical situation (4). You must be able to focus and filter clinical data in order to recognize what is most and least important so you can identify if an actual problem is present (3).

NANDA in Perspective

Though NANDA nursing diagnostic statements are taught as a taxonomy to establish nursing priorities, the use of NANDA alone can actually be a potential barrier to identify the current care priority when the status of the patient changes. Del Bueno found that new nurses were unable to exercise correct clinical judgment at a basic level to RESCUE (identify the problem and then intervene) their patient in a simulated scenario. The reason? Inappropriate use of NANDA nursing diagnostic statements to make them "fit" when there was a change in status (1).

For example, when a patient had a condition change consistent with a stroke, the nurse used the NANDA statement "alteration in sensory perception" or "alteration in nutrition." In another patient having symptoms consistent with a myocardial infarction, the nurse used "activity intolerance related to pain." Del Bueno summarizes her research findings with the following statement, "*Many inexperienced RN's also attempt to use a nursing diagnosis for the problem focus. Whatever the original intent for its use, the results are at best cumbersome and at worst laughable*" (1).

From my perspective, as a practicing nurse and nurse educator, NANDA remains relevant. NANDA should be seen as a foundational "FUNDAMENTAL" level of nurse thinking. Clinical reasoning is built upon this foundation to develop the ability to think like a nurse in practice when the status of your patient changes. Fundamental content remains relevant to the practicing nurse with advanced skills built upon this foundation in the second level of nursing education. In the same way, once NANDA is presented and situated in fundamentals, priority setting using clinical reasoning needs to be taught and then incorporated in the second level of nursing education.

You will use some NANDA nursing diagnostic statements regularly in practice. Some NANDA statements accurately capture the essence of a current problem such as "acute pain" and "fluid volume excess or deficit." One of the inherent weaknesses of NANDA is it is NOT how most nurses think in practice. Practical nurse thinking does not lend itself to a three-part NANDA nursing diagnostic statement with "related to" and "as evidenced by" that laid the foundation of care planning in nursing school. Prioritizing at the bedside is another limitation to the exclusive use of NANDA. How does the nurse establish a care priority when there is a change in status that has no NANDA statement? The following is a scenario that reflects this possibility:

Mrs. Smith is a forty-five year old woman who had an open hysterectomy earlier today. She is on a hydromorphone (Dilaudid) patient controlled analgesia (PCA) at 0.1 mg bolus every ten minutes. She has been complaining of increased pain and has been using her PCA every ten to twelve minutes for the past two hours. You enter the room to bring her clear liquid dinner tray and she appears to be sleeping comfortably with a RR of 16. Her O2 sats are 98 percent. You attempt to wake her, but she does not arouse to verbal stimuli. She does arouse with vigorous physical shaking but after a few seconds falls back to sleep. Recognizing that there is a problem, what is the NANDA statement that will accurately capture the essence of this change of status? How can the nurse establish a priority statement to guide the thinking that is needed to rescue this patient? Even if you had your NANDA Pocket Guide and could quickly review all 205 NANDA nursing diagnostic statements, you would not find a single statement that even comes close to identifying this scenario or making one "fit" the problem!

Instead of relying on a NANDA nursing diagnostic statement, the electronic medical record platform Epic incorporates in the nursing care plan the question that must be identified daily by the nurse, "What is your CARE PRIORITY?" This emphasis reflects the principle of clinical reasoning, which is to simply state the current problem or care priority that may or may not be a NANDA statement. By using clinical reasoning, you cluster the assessment data, which identifies the current problem and nursing priority. Once the priority problem is concisely stated, nursing interventions and expected outcomes flow and follow. Stating the problem in this scenario simply for what it is **"narcotic over sedation"** the interventions readily follow. The nurse would dilute naloxone (Narcan) 0. 4mg (1 mL) with 9 mL of saline and titrate 0.04-0.08 mg (1-2 mL) every couple of minutes until the patient's level of consciousness returned to the desirable level, and closely monitor neurologic status for any improvement to rescue this patient.

Key Components of Clinical Reasoning

What Is My Priority?

In any practice setting, but especially in acute care, the condition and status of your patient can change rapidly. The strength of clinical reasoning to clinical practice is that it emphasizes how to THINK IN ACTION and reason as a situation changes (4). The probability of a change in status is likely for any patient in your care and must be anticipated, especially in acute care. For the new nurse, the difficulty of setting care priorities is that all tasks and priorities seem to be of equal significance. Knowing which tasks are a priority is not always readily apparent because you may have difficulty seeing the big picture and identifying what is clinically significant. As a new nurse, you may tend to be task oriented and focused on what needs to be done, not necessarily what is most important.

In order to clinically reason in practice, one must be able to identify the most RELEVANT problem(s), which is essential for proper priority setting and good clinical judgment (3). In the clinical environment the nurse must know what assessments and tasks are most important to do FIRST. In addition, the nurse will have multiple patients. Who is seen first and why? Though there may be multiple tasks that need to be done, when a patient complains of chest pain or shortness of breath, will you recognize this as a priority and stop everything you are doing? I hope so! This reflects the flexibility the nurse must have in clinical practice and how priorities can quickly change.

Why?

You must be able to understand the "WHY" of all that you do for your patient. This includes the rationale for all medications you are administering, nursing interventions and even the physician plan of care and any new orders that have been written. Your clear UNDERSTANDING of the rationale for everything that is done in practice provides the foundation for SAFE patient care. If something does not make sense based on your best understanding of rationale, it must be questioned. This will be the challenge to you as a new nurse. There is still so much you do not know and need to know and your days will be busy. Make the most of any down time you may have to expand and develop your knowledge base so that you can build on your ability to understand rationale of everything that is done in clinical practice.

Trending to Rescue

Trending to rescue was addressed at length earlier, but I want to emphasize that it is also an essential component of clinical reasoning and thinking like a nurse in practice. You must be able to recognize SUBTLE changes in a patient's condition over time. It is the EARLY changes in a patient status that are subtle and, therefore, must be recognized before a problem progresses and an adverse outcome results or even death! The nurse must stay engaged and interpret the present clinical situation in comparing the present to what was last assessed (3). This includes the evaluation of any nursing interventions and the trending of all relevant assessment data and laboratory values. Remember that you are a knowledge worker and you must use this knowledge to put the pieces of the clinical puzzle together by identifying the patient's primary problem, current assessment data, and any trends that are concerning. When this is done, you will be able to recognize a problem early and take needed interventions to "RESCUE" your patient.

Clinical Reasoning Questions to Develop Nurse Thinking

I have created a template of clinical reasoning questions (see appendix J) that situate the components of clinical reasoning and how a nurse thinks in practice. These questions have been derived and adapted from the work of leading nurse educators such as Patricia Benner, Linda Caputi, Lisa Day, as well as my own observations from clinical experience. This template of clinical reasoning questions is used in every clinical reasoning case study in this book. This will allow you to PRACTICE NURSE THINKING in the safety of your own home. These same clinical reasoning questions will transfer to the clinical setting and will be used with every patient you care for. They are divided into a series of questions that must be formulated by the nurse before care is provided as well as questions that must be formulated and reflected during patient care. These clinical reasoning questions will lay the foundation to think like a nurse and provide safe, effective care in clinical practice!

Template of Clinical Reasoning Questions

Formulate and reflect on the following BEFORE providing care:

1. *What is the primary problem and what is the underlying cause /pathophysiology of this problem?*

2. *What clinical data **from the chart** is RELEVANT and needs to be trended because it is clinically significant?*

3. *What nursing priority will guide your plan of care?*

4. *What nursing interventions will you initiate based on this priority and what are the desired outcomes?*

5. *What body system(s) will you focus on based on your patient's primary problem or nursing care priority?*

6. *What is the worst possible/most likely complication(s) to anticipate based on the primary problem?*

7. What nursing assessments will you need to initiate to identify this complication if it develops?

Formulate and reflect on the following WHILE providing care:

8. What clinical assessment data did you *just collect* that is RELEVANT and needs to be TRENDED because it is clinically significant to detect a change in status?

9. Does your nursing priority or plan of care need to be modified in any way after assessing your patient?

10. After reviewing the primary care provider's note, what is the rationale for any new orders or changes made?

11. What educational/discharge priorities have you identified and how will you address them?

To promote your learning of this foundational template of clinical reasoning and thinking like a nurse in practice, let me briefly explain what is most important and relevant for each of these questions that you will use in practice:

1. *What is the primary problem and what is the underlying cause /pathophysiology of this problem?*

    This is typically going to be the admission medical problem or diagnosis. The most important aspect of this question is your ability to UNDERSTAND the pathophysiology of this illness or problem. You are going to routinely encounter diseases you barely remember covering in school or not at all. Make it a priority to promote your learning every day you practice by using the internet to research what you do not know. Emedicine.com is my favorite resource for this purpose. This is important to practice because when you have a clear understanding of what is taking place with your patient at a pathophysiologic level, your ability to think critically and clinically is developed and deepened.

2. *What clinical data from the chart is RELEVANT that needs to be trended because it is clinically significant?*

    One observation I have made, as a nurse educator, is that students will take as much time as you give them in the clinical setting to collect data on their patient from the medical record. The problem with this is that students and new nurses do not have an experiential base to recognize what clinical data is relevant and will, therefore, tend to write down any and everything that is present. The ability to filter clinical data and focus on what is RELEVANT is a work in progress, but this essential skill can also be practiced with the clinical reasoning case studies I have developed. For example, if you are caring for a patient with heart failure exacerbation, the diagnostic tests that are especially relevant and must be noted by the nurse include the K+, Mg+, creatinine, BNP, chest X-ray, and 12 lead EKG.

3. *What nursing priority will guide your plan of care?*

As stated earlier in this chapter, this may or may not be a NANDA nursing diagnostic statement. If we follow this same patient with heart failure exacerbation, NANDA statements of "fluid volume excess" and "impaired gas exchange" will be relevant. But if the status of this patient changes and is now having runs of ventricular tachycardia, a NANDA statement is not readily identifiable. Therefore simply stating the obvious (12 beat runs of ventricular tachycardia) and initiate needed interventions to rescue your patient is the essence of clinical reasoning.

4. *What nursing interventions will you initiate based on this priority and what are the desired outcomes?*

This is nothing new and is the essence of what you have done in writing care plans with specific nursing interventions and the expected outcome in nursing education. Though not situated in this question, you must also be able to identify the RATIONALE for every intervention that you initiate so that the "WHY" is understood and can determine if this intervention makes sense.

5. *What body system(s) will you focus on based on your patient's primary problem or nursing care priority?*

Though you perform a head to toe assessment for every patient you care for, you will focus and more thoroughly assess certain body systems that are relevant to their primary problem. If your patient is admitted with heart failure exacerbation, you will focus and more thoroughly assess the cardiovascular and respiratory body systems, but the GI system will likely not be as relevant. This is expected and is one practical way that your practice must be modified when you have multiple patients and only so much time.

6. *What is the worst possible/most likely complication(s) to anticipate based on the primary problem?*

This will be expanded later in this chapter under the heading "Looking for 'Jason'…the Worst Possible Complication."

7. *What nursing assessments will you need to initiate to identify this complication if it develops?*

This will be expanded later in this chapter under the heading, "Looking for 'Jason'…the Worst Possible Complication."

8. What clinical assessment data did you just collect that is RELEVANT and needs to be TRENDED because it is clinically significant to detect a change in status?

This is an important aspect of practice that was addressed in chapter two. Remember that this is not just recognizing what data is relevant, but also consistently comparing the data you received in report and what is in the chart with the assessment data you personally collected. Has anything changed? Were any of the findings unexpected and require further assessment or an SBAR to the physician? Because patients rarely stay static, but can quickly change, this aspect of nurse VIGILENCE is what is required to "RESCUE" your patient if there is a change in status.

9. Does your nursing priority or plan of care need to be modified in any way after assessing your patient?

Have you ever experienced the frustration of your written care plan NOT reflecting the current needs of your patient when you care for him or her? This is a reality of clinical practice and change is the one thing you can always count on in caring for your patients as well as in healthcare!

10. After reviewing the primary care provider's note, what is the rationale for any new orders or changes made?

Though we are not primary care providers, it is essential to understand the essence of the primary care provider's plan of care and their rationale for any modifications they have made by adding or discontinuing certain medications. The daily progress note or most recent documentation of the primary care provider is a "must read" by the nurse to clearly understand their priorities and benefit from their perspective on the patient you are caring for.

11. What educational/discharge priorities have you identified and how will you address them?

The professional nurse is also an educator. I will go into more detail in the next chapter on this very topic, but every patient you care for has a need for education to promote his/her health and care. Make it a priority to identify what his needs are and take the initiative to educate. You cannot teach what you do not know well. This is another reason why it is so important to understand and be knowledgeable about all aspects of your patient and his illness and medications he is taking.

Looking for "JASON"...the Worst Possible Complication

Because of its importance and relevance to practice, the following two questions (6, 7) from the template of clinical reasoning will be explained in further detail.

6. What is the worst possible/most likely complication(s) to anticipate based on primary problem?

7. What nursing assessments will you need to initiate to identify this complication if it develops?

Do any of you remember "Jason" from the original *Friday the 13th* slasher/horror movies from the 1980's? A group of teenagers are murdered one by one while attempting to reopen an abandoned campground. Since I graduated from high school in 1981, and the first of many in this series started in 1980, I remember all too well the classic ending from the original. Only Alice survived the terrifying night at Camp Crystal Lake and as morning came, she was on a small boat in the middle of the lake. All is calm and quiet, the birds are singing and she has no reason to be concerned. But out of nowhere Jason leaps out of the water and grabs Alice and takes her down…but it was only a dream and a movie. No reason to fear and look for Jason any longer, right? WRONG! Do you realize that "JASON" is still out there and lurks around the corner of every clinical setting? Who is Jason? He is a metaphor for the worst possible/most likely complication your patient may experience. You must apply your knowledge and identify the most likely complication for every patient you care for. Jason is still very deadly, but he has new names such as sepsis, septic shock, post-op bleed, respiratory distress, and cardiac arrest, to name only a few.

Clinical vigilance is required to keep "Jason" from impacting your patient and experiencing an adverse outcome. If you are intentionally looking for him, you will recognize the worst possible complications before it is too late. It is only when the nurse has lost this sense of vigilance and forgets that "Jason" is still out there that complications go unnoticed until it is often too late. I have seen from my own clinical experience that any post-op patient is at risk for septic or hypovolemic shock; these are especially deadly when not recognized EARLY.

Sepsis is one of the most common "Jason's" and hides early with subtle changes such as a low-grade temperature, slight hypotension, and tachycardia. When the nurse does not recognize the significance of these findings, the tachycardia will persist as Jason continues to have his way. It is only when Jason is RECOGNIZED, that his power to destroy is broken and your patient can be RESCUED from a likely adverse outcome.

Looking for "JASON"

In order to rescue a patient from a deteriorating change of status, it must be vigilantly looked for. EARLY signs and symptoms must be identified so that the complication is not allowed to needlessly progress. The pathophysiology of this possible complication must be understood. This provides the needed deep thinking and mastery of relevant content to your practice specialty. By doing this consistently, you will develop a needed heightened vigilance which is essential to practice.

When analyzing a new graduate's ability to think critically, especially in the context of a change of status, Dorothy Del Bueno identified the following four questions that must be answered so that a change of status is RECOGNIZED by the nurse. You will see that there is some overlap and correlation to these questions and the essence of clinical reasoning. Following each question are additional subtopics that will further practically situate this content:

1. **Can you recognize there is a problem? Until the problem is recognized, no action will be taken.**
    - Recognize what clinical data is RELEVANT.
    - Identify medical/nursing PRIORITY.
    - Identify what is the most likely WORST POSSIBLE COMPLICATION for your patient.
    - Intentional vigilance to be LOOKING for this complication and trending over time all RELEVANT clinical data and required assessments.

2. **Can the nurse manage the problem safely and effectively, recognizing scope of practice?**
    - Nursing interventions to initiate based on current problem once identified.

3. **Does the nurse have a relative sense of URGENCY?**
    - Lack of clinical experience is a barrier for the nurse to develop this sense of urgency but will come in time. I have seen new graduate nurses have a patient with a status change of sepsis, yet have no sense of urgency when his BP has dropped to 70/30!

4. **Does the nurse take the right action for the right reason?**
    - RATIONALE for nursing/medical interventions once problem is identified.
    - Contact the physician promptly to initiate needed interventions (1).

Most Common "JASON's"

At the hospital where I practice there is a "Rapid Response Team" (RRT) that rounds the hospital 24/7, circulating and responding to the call by a nurse that identifies a possible change in status that may indicate a need to rescue. If you practice in a different setting, make it a priority to ask the experienced nurses what are the most common changes of status that must be anticipated. Based on statistical data compiled as to why a RRT is paged where I practice, you can anticipate these most common changes of status in your patient in the acute care setting.

Top five in order of frequency:

I. Chest pain

Regardless of your practice setting, the nurse will need to evaluate and assess chest pain in such diverse settings as phone triage, the outpatient setting, community health clinics, and even as school nurses. In acute care, this is by far the most common reason an RRT is paged. The good news is that most chest pain is NOT cardiac, but it could still be a potential problem because pneumonia and a pulmonary embolus can also cause this complaint. If your patient has a complaint of chest pain, it is essential to perform the following assessments to differentiate cardiac vs. noncardiac chest pain. If available in your practice setting, a 12 lead EKG is standard practice to determine if there are new changes consistent with ischemia. What are these changes? In early ischemia, the T waves that are normally rounded and upright may be flattened or inverted. The ST segment after the QRS complex may be either elevated or depressed more than 1 mm.

In addition to the EKG, you must look at your patient! Does he look as if he is in distress? Has his color changed from pink, warm, and dry to pale, cool, and diaphoretic? Is he anxious, restless, or are other subtle but apparent changes present? If so, then this validates his current complaint is likely more serious and could be cardiac. In addition to an EKG, the following nursing assessments must be implemented to put this clinical puzzle together and differentiate what is driving this complaint:

Take a deep breath

- If taking a deep breath causes the pain to dramatically increase, then this chest pain is most likely noncardiac. But pleurisy, pneumonia, and a pulmonary embolus also cause pleuritic chest pain. So the next assessment needed that will help clarify the cause of this chest pain is palpation.

Palpate the area of pain for reproducible tenderness

- Gently but firmly palpate the location of where the pain is present. If the pain is reproducible with palpation, this is most likely noncardiac and is likely pleurisy, an inflammation of the pleura that is non-emergent.

Location of the pain
- There are gender differences of cardiac chest pain. For example, women tend to have a higher likelihood of nonclassic symptoms that include epigastric pain as well as referred pain with no anterior chest pain. For most patients though, cardiac chest pain will be anterior chest pain in a large, general area of the chest. If the pain is localized to a very small area that the patient can point to, this is typically NOT associated with angina.

Presence of other complaints consistent with cardiac ischemia
- In addition to the primary location of the chest pain, cardiac chest pain typically consists of referred pain to the neck, back, jaw, or arms. It is important for the nurse to determine if this referred pain is present or not with the primary complaint of chest pain (Looking back in your pathophysiology book will explain the rationale for why cardiac pain can be referred to a different region of the body).
- Shortness of breath (SOB) is also a common component of cardiac chest pain related to coronary artery disease and myocardial ischemia. It is important for the nurse to determine if SOB is present as well.

Length of pain
- This will help differentiate cardiac from noncardiac chest pain because angina will typically last longer than five minutes. If the patient reports that this pain lasts for just a few seconds at a time, or less than a minute, this pain is likely noncardiac.

Character of pain
- It is important to distinguish if the nature or character of this pain is similar to any prior history of heartburn or GERD. If it is, this again is likely non-cardiac. Cardiac chest pain is most commonly a diffuse pressure, tightness, squeezing, or achiness.

In order to cement your knowledge of this content, I have created this table. Use your textbook as well as the content of this chapter to develop this table on your own.

	Noncardiac Chest Pain	Cardiac Chest Pain
Physical Appearance		
Deep Breath		
Palpation		
Location of Pain		
Referred Pain		
Length of Pain		
Nature of Pain		

II. **Increased respiratory distress/O2 sats <90%**

If your patient is complaining of shortness of breath and/or has decreased oxygenation, immediate intervention and relevant assessments are required by the nurse. Use the same principle of: "How does my patient look?" If he looks like he is in distress, he most likely is! In addition to general appearance, the following are the most relevant assessments that must be closely trended over time:

Respiratory rate

- Rate > 20 is a clinical RED FLAG and likely represents distress, anxiety, or both!

Heart rate

- Rate >100 is a clinical RED FLAG and will be elevated with physiologic distress caused by sympathetic nervous system stimulation.

O2 saturation

- Saturation <90% is a clinical RED FLAG that is reflecting hypoxia in a non-COPD patient. With any complaint of SOB, immediately obtain the oxygen saturation to determine the baseline with this change of status, and then administer supplemental oxygenation and titrate to oxygen saturation greater than 92 percent.

Breath sounds:

- Posterior auscultation FIRST if possible, then anterior. There is less subcutaneous fat posterior and able to detect adventitious breath sounds more readily. Listen carefully to all lobes especially the bases. Compare each lobe right to left. Rales or crackles typically represent fluid seen in the alveoli with heart failure. Rhonchi is most commonly seen with secretions and pneumonia. Wheezing or very-diminished aeration is typical with asthmatic or COPD exacerbation. However, an audible wheeze may be present in heart failure due to fluid in the alveoli causing bronchial constriction. This is referred to as cardiac asthma.

III. Patient fall

The most important PRIORITY is the MECHANISM OF INJURY related to the fall. If the patient fell in such a way that he has complaints of pain, or may have hit his head, he may require cervical spine immobilization by the RRT, or a properly trained nurse. He must be kept perfectly still until this immobilization takes place and a cervical spine injury is ruled out. Additional relevant neurologic assessments that can be made by the nurse include:

- *Level of consciousness (LOC)*
- *Movement of all extremities*
- *Numbness, weakness, tingling in any extremity*

IV. Hypotension

This can be caused by many things, but the most common is fluid volume loss/deficit related to bleeding, dehydration, or sepsis. If you have been carefully trending the systolic blood pressure and it is running 30+ points lower than baseline, or if the systolic blood pressure is less than 100, this is a clinical RED FLAG that must be recognized by the nurse. So, if the systolic blood pressure has been trending 130–140 consistently and now you are 100–110, though not less than 100, this is still a RED FLAG and you must step back and ask WHY?

With any shock or volume depleted state, the earliest compensatory response by the body is to increase heart rate in response to decreased cardiac output. Remember CO=SVxHR from A&P? The finding of a low blood pressure with tachycardia demands an immediate response. When a low blood pressure trend is identified, the following priority assessments must be clustered and trended with the current blood pressure to determine the most likely complication that is beginning to manifest.

General appearance

- Does he or she appear in any distress or is the patient tolerating the decrease in BP? You need to determine if he is unstable with this finding or not. This will help determine the urgency you need to have in this clinical situation.

Skin

- If he or she is in distress with sympathetic nervous system stimulation, he will likely be pale, cool, and diaphoretic. In early shock, his extremities will be cooler when compared centrally by touching his forehead. If your patient is cool centrally and this is a new finding, this is an urgent situation and must be recognized as such.

Pulses

- The pulses must be taken while assessing the coolness or warmth of the extremities. If the pulses are already more difficult to palpate than a prior assessment, this is a critical RED FLAG that most likely represents a shock state as the body shunts volume centrally from the periphery. Don't forget to auscultate and palpate together to notice any differences.

Temperature

- A complete set of vital signs, including the temperature, is essential with a low blood pressure. The most common complication that must be ruled out is SEPSIS. An elevated temperature with a low blood pressure is a classic finding with sepsis, and with the elderly it is not uncommon to have a low temperature less than 96.5. This is a clinical RED FLAG that must be recognized by the nurse as well.

Heart rate

- The expected physiologic response to volume depletion and a low blood pressure is tachycardia, which is an early sign of physiologic compensatory mechanisms. If the patient is NOT tachycardic with a low blood pressure, it is important for the nurse to look at his daily medications. What medication will influence the finding of a normal heart rate in a shock state? Any beta-blocker will prevent the heart rate from being elevated even when the sympathetic nervous system is activated!

Respiratory rate
- It is important to note the respiratory rate because of its relationship to shock. If your patient is in any form of progressive shock state, he will likely be tachypneic. This must be noted if present or not.

Blood pressure
- This is obvious, and the most important finding related to blood pressure is the current trend and what direction it is going. Remember that even if the SBP is >100 but has dropped by 30+ mm/Hg recently from prior assessments, this is a clinical concern that must be recognized by the nurse.

V. Change in LOC or neurologic status

Whenever there is a change in neurologic status, it is important for the nurse to determine the most obvious reason. For example, if your patient just received a dose of IV hydromorphone (Dilaudid) and now is more lethargic and difficult to arouse, narcotic sedation is the most likely cause. Instead of beginning with the assumption that this is a stroke, begin with this obvious assumption and cluster your data from there. Though narcotic over sedation is the most common reason for a clinical change and altered level of consciousness, the nurse must also be vigilant for the possibility of a stroke with any of the following NEW assessment findings:

Facial droop
- This is always a clinical RED FLAG, and, if present, a complete neuro assessment must be immediately initiated. This finding can be subtle with just the corner of the mouth level while the other side moves or is elevated in comparison. If you are suspicious that this is present, simply have the patient smile BIG and show their teeth and it will be clear if a droop is present or not.

Hemiparesis
- Weakness on either side of the body that may or may not involve both upper and lower extremities is also a clinical RED FLAG. For example, it is not

uncommon for an upper extremity to have weakness, but the lower extremity of the impaired side to have normal strength.

Slurred speech
- If the patient has slurred speech or expressive or receptive aphasia this is a clinical RED FLAG that is consistent with a stroke. The nurse must recognize the significance and the need to make this patient NPO until this has been ruled out.

Confusion or disorientation
- This finding can be generalized to other problems besides a stroke, but if present and no medications have been given that would alter his level of consciousness, then this becomes more concerning and a thorough neurologic assessment must be initiated by the nurse.

Cincinnati Pre-Hospital Stroke Scale

A simple, focused neurologic assessment that can be done quickly to determine the possibility of a stroke is called the "Cincinnati Pre-Hospital Stroke Scale." It tests three signs for abnormal findings which may indicate that the patient is having a stroke. Though designed for emergency medical staff in pre-hospital care, it can guide the nurse in any clinical setting if there is cause for concern with any new neurologic changes. Patients with one of these three findings as a new event have a 72 percent probability of an ischemic stroke. If all three findings are present, the probability of an acute stroke is more than 85 percent. Even if you are not confident in your comprehensive neuro-assessment skills, this will simplify what you NEED TO KNOW in this context of a change in neurological status.

Three Essential Assessments

1. **Facial droop:** Have the person smile or show his or her teeth. If one side doesn't move as well as the other so it seems to droop, this is clinically significant and a possible stroke.
   a. *Normal:* Both sides of face move equally.
   b. *Abnormal:* One side of face does not move as well as the other.

2. **Arm drift:** Have the person close his or her eyes and hold his or her arms straight out in front, palms up for about ten seconds. If one arm does not move, or one arm winds up drifting down more than the other, this is clinically significant and a possible stroke.

a. *Normal:* Both arms stay level and do NOT drift.
b. *Abnormal:* One arm does not move, or one arm drifts down compared with the other side.

3. **Speech:** Have the person say, "You can't teach an old dog new tricks," or some other simple, familiar saying. If the person slurs the words, gets some words wrong, or is unable to speak, this is clinically significant and a possible stroke.
    a. *Normal:* Patient uses correct words with no slurring.
    b. *Abnormal:* Slurred or inappropriate words or mute (5).

FAST is an acronym that will also help to situate this important content on a neurological change of status using the same assessment data used in the Cincinnati Pre-Hospital Stroke Scale (6).

- **F**ace
    - **F**acial droop present?
- **A**rm
    - **A**rm drift?
- **S**peech
    - **S**lurred or aphasic?
- **T**ime
    - **T**ime is of the essence if any of these symptoms present! Get medical assistance immediately!

Additional Resources:

- Book: *Clinical Wisdom and Interventions in Acute and Critical Care, Second Edition: A Thinking-in-Action Approach* by Patricia Benner, Patricia Hooper Kyriakidis, & Daphne Stannard

Building the "Living" House of Professional Practice

Chapter 4: Supporting Structures: Safety, Education, and Expert Practice

---

Though a house may appear complete with the foundation dug, the walls built, and the roof completed, there are additional supporting structures that are needed so the home stays strong, resistant, and resilient over the years. The "living" house of professional practice is no different; and the supporting structures that will keep your practice strong and solid over the life of your career are the threads of safety and education. What makes the living house of professional practice truly unique and alive is what you decide to pour and put into it. This personal, living component of the house is your decision to commit yourself to be the best that you can be and a desire to grow over time into an expert practitioner.

Safety Defined

Safety is also a competency of QSEN that is defined as when the nurse "minimizes risk of harm to patients and providers through both system effectiveness and individual performance" (1). This definition is important to practice because it addresses the "systems" that may have clearly contributed to any nurse error. Changing the confusing labeling of medications is an example of this more global approach to safety in clinical practice. The attitudes that the nurse must have to lay a foundation of safety in clinical practice is to value a nurse's own role in preventing errors, value vigilance and monitoring of one's performance, as well as other members of the healthcare team, and recognizing one's physical limits of safe performance (1). Be vigilant of the impact that rotating shifts and picking up extra hours can have on affecting your ability to be safe!

Essential Safety Assessments

Once you have received report at the change of shift, each patient on your assignment is now your responsibility. In addition to the obvious responsibilities and nursing priorities related to their care, you are also responsible for any inherited errors that may be present even though you were not directly responsible for them. In order to provide safe care in every aspect related to your patient, I have found the following to be a relevant safety "checklist" of essential assessments in the acute care setting to review as you enter each room of your patient for the first time (modify this list as needed depending on your clinical practice setting):

General

Tab alarms

- Make sure that any device that is related to preventing a patient fall is properly working. Tab alarms must be properly secured to the patient in order for them to release and alarm.

Level of bed/side rails

- Be sure to note if the bed is down at the lowest position as well as the side rails being up or down depending on the need and concern for safety.

Room order.

- Though the room may have been a mess when you come on, it is not okay to leave it that way! A room that is clean and in order is a room that promotes a healing environment. Therefore, this should be a priority for the nurse. Do what is needed to bring order and cleanliness to every patient's room. Remember that the floor of any care setting is obviously dirty and contaminated. One of my pet peeves is the frequency I find sequential compression device (SCD's) sleeves that go around the lower legs of the patient on the floor when they are not in use! Do not be that nurse. Keep them off the floor and as clean as possible!
  - *Fresh water.* Make sure that the patient has fresh water and all old trays and food that may no longer be safe is removed

IV Assessments

Assessment of IV site

- *Make it a priority to determine if the IV site is patent or not.*
  - From my clinical experience I have seen an IV patent and just a few minutes later can be obviously infiltrated. The most common signs that you will see clinically with IV infiltration is leakage of fluid at the insertion site, pain, and obvious swelling distal to the insertion site.

- *Is IV well secured?*
  - It is not uncommon for a peripheral IV to be poorly secured or the tape peeling off when you assess it for the first time. It is not good for you or the patient to have this IV pull out and need to be restarted if it did not have to be. Make it a priority to carry tape with you and secure it immediately as needed.

- *Is IV dressing intact?*
  - The clear Tegaderm® dressing can peel on the edges to such a degree that the insertion site is compromised. This is especially important to determine site integrity with any type of central line because of the risk of sepsis. If peeling on the edges but site intact, reinforce with tape. If site compromised, change dressing per hospital protocol ASAP!

IV fluids

- *Determine that the IV solution is exactly what is ordered on the Medication Administration Record (MAR).*
  - A common error that I have observed is related to the similarities of many IV fluids such as D5 0.9% NS vs. D5 0.45% NS.

IV rate

- *Confirm that the IV rate is exactly what is ordered on the MAR.*
  - These rates can change frequently and might have been missed by the prior nurse. Double-check the MAR with the correct rate as an essential safety check at the beginning of your shift.

Oxygen Assessments

- This is especially important if the patient has a history of COPD and is on a specific flow rate at home. This flow rate must be the same to ensure adequate oxygenation.
- If there is no specific rate that the physician has ordered but instead has an order to keep oxygenation greater than 92 percent, once a complete assessment of your patient has been made, do not hesitate to wean and decrease this rate if the oxygenation is greater than the minimum percentage ordered to advance the plan of care. For example, I have cared for many patients who are on oxygen per nasal cannula with O2 sats of 100 percent who had been documented for 2-3 shifts at 100 percent and were able to be promptly weaned to room air with no significant drop in O2 sats.

Naso-gastric (NG) Tube Assessments

NG to correct suction

- *You must confirm from the chart and physician order the correct amount of suction.*
    - The most common settings are low continuous suction, or low intermittent suction. Determine from the suction unit on the wall if the correct suction is currently applied.

Correct placement

- *Determine the correct centimeter markings from the prior assessment and recheck to make sure nothing has changed.*
    - Follow your hospital or institution's policy for verifying placement once the tube has been established. After I have confirmed placement, I have found it beneficial to place a pen mark just below the tape that is attached to the tube so I have a visual identifier every time I enter the room that the tube is still properly placed.

Properly secured

- This is the same principle that is also essential for a peripheral IV. It is not uncommon for the tape or securement device to become moist and the tube is barely holding on to the nose. It is also important to make sure that the tape that is attached to the tube below the nostril is holding the tube firmly and not allowing it to slide. You must physically grasp the tube to see if it has any movement back and forth. I have seen tubes appear to be in place but because this aspect of the tube is not secure the tube can slowly be sliding out. I have encountered this problem in practice quite often.

Enteral formula correct

- Same principle under IV fluids.

Tube feeding at correct rate

- Same principle under IV rate.

Chest Tube Assessments

Chest tubes banded

- To simplify my assessment of a patient with a chest tube, I start with the patient and work my way down to the water seal chamber. My first priority is to make sure the chest tube has the white thin plastic "zip tie" bands where it is secured to the tubing that is coming from the water seal unit. It must be secured on each side of the connector. If this band is missing the chest tube could become disconnected and a pneumothorax would result. This is a good example of how a LITTLE THING can become a BIG THING!

Chest tube secured

- Chest tubes are painful if they move excessively. Therefore, make it a priority to securely tape it to the chest, ideally with foam tape.

Crepitus

- While you are at the patient's side, gently palpate the chest at the insertion site for the presence of crepitus. The significance of crepitus is that it is air leaking into the subcutaneous tissue and the extent of crepitus must be identified if present. It is not typically a critical event but the physician should be notified if present and documented in the chart. Crepitus has the potential to compromise the patient's airway. Patients have developed an "Incredible Hulk" type of look caused by the crepitus under the skin! Crepitus can create a medical emergency by occluding the airway by soft tissue swelling that can radiate from the chest tube insertion site, so don't minimize this problem if it presents!

Correct suction

- With a wet suction water seal chamber, the correct amount of suction is determined by the amount of water that is present in the suction chamber. It is not uncommon for this to be less than the typical -20 cm of suction. If it is low, add enough sterile water to bring it up to -20 cm.
- Newer models of the Atrium water seal units are dry suction and no longer require water level to determine suction. They are also completely quiet and make no "bubbling" noises like an aquarium. Instead there is an orange bellows that is fully inflated and sticks out horizontally when proper suction is applied. Either way make sure there is proper suction going to the unit!

Presence of air leak

- Determine the presence of an air leak by looking for small bubbles that are present in the water seal chamber. The water level commonly fluctuates with inspiration and expiration but no bubbles should be seen. If an air leak is present and this is new, as long as there is no respiratory distress from the patient, this is not a critical event but the physician should be notified and documented in the chart.

- It is more concerning to have a continuous air leak than an air leak that is present intermittently or only with a deep cough. Note the characteristics of the air leak and document this and report to the primary care provider as needed.

Nurse as Educator

As a new nurse you may be reluctant to embrace the role of an educator. You have just graduated and recognize the limitations of what you know and how much more you need to know. I want to encourage you to embrace the role and responsibility of an educator! If you do this well, you will empower your patients and their families by helping them to understand their illness and take responsibility to do their part to promote and maintain their health. If teaching was not done or was not performed well, they may experience a decline in health and be needlessly readmitted. Knowledge is power, and as a "knowledge worker" (2) you must use this power to your patient's advantage. Your patient and his family should be considered a partner in care and work together as able in the clinical setting. As partners, patients are now expected to learn about their own health to be able to participate in healthcare decisions. The goal of patient education is to assist a patient and his family to learn about his healthcare to improve his own health. By following the two principles of simplicity and reinforcement you will be empowered to embrace this responsibility!

Simplicity
1. Teach the simple concepts about a topic first, and then move to the more complex concepts.
2. Use language that your patient will find easy to understand and avoid medical terminology whenever possible. Consider the age, level of education and current profession to determine the level at which to teach (3).

Reinforcement
1. Teach the one concept you want your patient to learn FIRST.
2. Ask your patient to restate what you have taught, so you can be sure he understood.
3. Use visual aids for teaching; using several senses improves learning.
4. Always use written educational materials for the client to take home if available (3).

Additional principles that I have found helpful to promote patient engagement and meaningful learning include the following:
- Include the FAMILY as much as possible in education. The spouse or significant other is likely going to be needed to reinforce what you are teaching once the patient is home.

- Define the priority educational needs and desired outcome of education.
- Minimize any/all distractions and teach at a time that is best for the patient.
- If there are relevant risk factors present that must be managed to promote health and disease progression, be sure that they are taught and understood.
- Assess what the patient/family already knows and what must be REINFORCED.
- Assess for any barriers to learning such as language, level of education, HOH, and motivation.
- When administering medications, assess knowledge by asking the question, "Do you know what this is for?" and if the patient is unable to answer, you can reinforce or choose to address any knowledge deficits another time.

So You Want to Be an Expert?

Patricia Benner, whose work is widely cited in this text, is best known for her early nursing research that led to her book, *From Novice to Expert: Clinical Excellence and Power in Clinical Practice*. This work detailed how nurses progress, develop skills and understanding of patient care over time. The five levels of nurse proficiency in practice Benner identified are novice, advanced beginner, competent, proficient, and expert (4).

Summary of Novice to Expert

The relevance of Benner's framework is that it defines definite steps and levels of clinical progression and the characteristics of nursing practice at each level. To practically situate her framework, you began nursing school as a "novice." You had no prior clinical experience as a nurse and because of this were unable to recognize what clinical data was relevant and when an exception to standards of care was in order (4). For example, knowing that normal O2 sats are >95% and your patient with end-stage COPD has O2 sats of 90%, which is likely their normal, the novice will likely not recognize this exception because of the lack of clinical context and inflexible rule governed behavior. As a graduate nurse you are now on the second level of proficiency which is "advanced beginner." You will tend to be strongly TASK oriented, and will not readily recognize priorities and what task is most important to do first (4).

For example, when you see your patient for the first time and you have to do VS, assessment, room order, and medications, recognizing which task is the priority is not always readily apparent (4). To become "competent," the third level of proficiency typically requires two to three YEARS of experience in the same clinical area (4). This nurse knows what needs to be done and is able to set needed priorities to efficiently organize and manage the day.

At a minimum, the nurse must uphold and perform the standards of safe practice. To progress through these stages requires TIME IN PRACTICE or, in other words, there is no substitute for clinical experience! But time alone will not make you an expert clinician. To progress to be an expert nurse, you must be motivated and guided by the DESIRE to BE excellent in what you do in practice. Excellent practice at its very root is SELF-MOTIVATING (5). Pursuing certification in your desired nursing specialty, even if it is not required, is an example of professional growth that will likely lead to expert practice over time.

Centrality of Caring

Caring remains central for the nurse to progress and develop to become an expert practitioner. The heightened level of INVOLVEMENT that caring represents is foundational to expert nursing practice (6). CARING is what makes the nurse notice what interventions are most effective as well as identifying subtle signs of improvement or deterioration. Benner studied what characteristics made expert nurses effective in practice. She identified that knowledge and technique were not enough; caring is an essential component that will lay the foundation to become an expert in nursing practice (5).

Progression vs. Regression

An important point to consider as you examine each of these levels of proficiency is to realize they are not static, but can progress or regress over time. If the nurse is engaged and motivated in practice, she will progress with time and experience to an expert level. But what happens if that same nurse experiences depression, stress of a divorce, or burnout in the current position? Is it realistic to maintain the same level of motivation and engagement under these circumstances? For most it is not and regression to a lower level of proficiency is inevitable. This is where it becomes essential to form the professional discipline and habit of reflection. It is possible to regress and not realize it! This is why the house of professional practice is living, alive, and evolves over time. Depending on the amount of energy and passion you bring to your practice, this will directly reflect how "alive" your house really is.

Additional Resources:

- Book: *From Novice to Expert: Excellence and Power in Clinical Nursing Practice* by Patricia Benner

Part II: Practical Preparation for Practice

Chapter 5: Putting It All Together: Clinical Reasoning Case Studies

It is now time for the equivalent of the final examination to prepare you for professional practice. Everything that you have learned in nursing education and in this book will now be put to the test through the use of clinical reasoning case studies. These case studies are unlike anything you have likely used in nursing education. The clinical reasoning questions in these case studies are open-ended. NO MULTIPLE CHOICE answers to choose from! You either know it or you don't! Do you have the option to "choose" the best current nursing priority or intervention in clinical practice?

The case studies that I have created begin with a realistic clinical scenario and the questions that follow provide a systematic TEMPLATE of NURSE THINKING that experienced nurses' use every day in practice that will lay a foundation of thinking like a nurse in practice. By working through a clinical reasoning case study that has the same template of clinical reasoning questions, you will PRACTICE nurse thinking. Other unique strengths of these case studies are that they emphasize the same key components that the NCLEX utilizes to assess student learning. If you have not taken the NCLEX, these case studies will COMPLEMENT any other review programs because they situate the following KEY NCLEX principles that are also relevant to clinical practice:

- APPLICATION of content/concepts to the bedside.
- PRIORITY SETTING based on the unique scenario.
- Clinical data RELEVANT to this scenario.
- RATIONALE for nursing interventions and physician orders.

Each case study has a similar structure that begins with a concise clinical scenario and patient story that unfolds gradually with initial VS, nursing assessment data, lab results, and physician orders. You will need to identify RELEVANT clinical data and rationale in the scenario, as well as identify nursing priorities with needed interventions. You will state the rationale for physician orders and plan of care. Because these case studies mirror clinical realities in practice, you will be able to readily transfer what you learn from these case studies to the bedside.

To promote your learning, I encourage you to WORK TOGETHER with other students or graduate nurses if possible. It has been shown that collaboration on clinical reasoning content promotes learning as you dialogue over the open-ended responses to come to the best clinical response to the scenario.

Choose a topic that is currently a weakness so that you can make it your strength! Print up the blank student version. Work through the case study and use textbook or web-based resources as needed to complete to the best of your ability. If you are unable to complete every question, no problem! Each case study also has a thorough and well-developed answer key that I have written in a casual style that is NOT like reading a textbook! The correct answers are supplied, but more importantly, thoroughly developed RATIONALE founded in my own observations from clinical practice to promote your learning that will translate over to your clinical practice.

To give you the opportunity to promote your learning of sepsis and to PRACTICE NURSE THINKING, I have included Sepsis: Unfolding Clinical Reasoning Case Study in this book. Sepsis is now the number one reason for hospital admissions and one of the most common reasons a patient experiences a change of status in the clinical setting. The related topics of pathophysiology, fluids and electrolytes, and acid-base balance are most effectively learned with a context in order to see why it is relevant. Therefore sepsis must be UNDERSTOOD and more importantly RECOGNIZED before it is too late.

I also created a SYNTHESIS case study on respiratory arrest due to narcotic over sedation that degenerates into a full cardiac arrest. What are your nursing priorities when you assess your patient and he is unresponsive and has no spontaneous respiratory effort or pulse? This case study will allow you to PRACTICE basic life support (BLS) as well as advanced cardiac life support (ACLS) life-saving interventions to help prepare you for this possibility in clinical practice. Arterial blood gas (ABG) interpretation and lab value interpretation are also situated to promote your understanding of acid-base in this scenario.

If you would like to DEEPEN your knowledge further, I have created a special package of ten med/surg case studies that were chosen because they complement one another as well as avoid repetition of similar content. Together, these clinical reasoning studies will lay a strong foundation of the most important and RELEVANT concepts to practice.

These ten case studies can be purchased separately on my website by clicking each link below. This will also provide additional details of the clinical scenario and content/concepts that are included for you to preview. You may also purchase at a significant discount all ten case studies when they are bundled together!

Cardiac
1. Heart Failure/Acute Renal Failure–Unfolding Reasoning
2. Acute Coronary Syndrome/Acute MI–Unfolding Reasoning
3. Atrial Fibrillation Rapid Reasoning

Respiratory
4. COPD/Pneumonia–Rapid Reasoning

GI
5. Small Bowel Obstruction–Rapid

Neuro
6. CVA–Unfolding Reasoning–Rapid Reasoning

Pediatrics
7. Gastroenteritis w/Severe Dehydration–Rapid Reasoning

F&E
8. Diabetic Ketoacidosis/Chronic Renal Failure–Unfolding Reasoning

Surgical
9. Spinal Surgery: Day of Surgery–Unfolding Reasoning

Final Synthesis
10. Synthesis: Cardiac Arrest–Unfolding Reasoning

MORE Clinical Reasoning Case Studies to Develop Nurse Thinking…

If you do not have the time or energy for doing ten case studies (though I strongly recommend it!) but would rather pick and choose, I have created three levels of clinical reasoning case studies that have a similar template of clinical reasoning questions. These studies can be purchased through my website KeithRN.com. For anyone who has purchased this book, you can acquire any clinical reasoning case study on my website and save 50 percent by using the coupon code at checkout: "think."

The "Rapid Reasoning" and "Unfolding Reasoning" case studies are the levels that I recommend for advanced nursing students or graduate nurses because of the depth of content and emphasis of clinical reasoning. See below for further distinctives of each clinical reasoning activity. By going to my website KeithRN.com, you can access each tab, obtain further information and see the variety of topics currently available. I am creating new case studies regularly, so check back frequently!

- Rapid Reasoning
    - Clinical scenario complete with chief complaint, past medical history, initial VS, nursing assessment and lab values.
    - Clinical reasoning questions that follow provide a template for "nurse thinking" that transfers learning to the clinical setting.
    - Short/condensed "just right" clinical reasoning activity.

- Unfolding Reasoning
    - Once the clinical scenario is presented, it unfolds and has a status change that requires the nurse to interpret clinical data, make a correct clinical interpretation and judgment, and then evaluate the clinical response to determine if the patient has improved or not. This mirrors the realities of what the nurse will likely experience in clinical practice.
    - Up to twice as long when compared to Rapid Reasoning.

- Fundamental Reasoning
    - Emphasis is on identifying clinical relationships (see beginning of chapter 3) that will develop critical thinking and lay the foundation for higher level nurse thinking.
    - Ideally suited for fundamental/first year level nursing content.
    - Incorporates pharmacology, nursing process, identifying relevant clinical data, and priority setting.
    - Some aspects of clinical reasoning are introduced but is geared for the fundamental level nursing student, though a second year student MAY find them helpful.

Unfolding Clinical Reasoning Case Study:
Sepsis: STUDENT VERSION
I. Data Collection

Chief complaint/History of Present Illness:

Mrs. Kelly is an 82 year old woman who has been feeling more fatigued for the last three days and has had a fever the last twenty-four hours. She reports painful, burning sensation when she urinates as well as frequency of urination the last week. Her daughter became concerned and brought her to the emergency department (ED) when she did not know what day it was. She is mentally alert with no history of confusion.

Personal/Social History:

Mrs. Kelly lives independently in a senior apartment. She is widowed and has two daughters who are active and involved in her life.

What data is RELEVANT that must be recognized as clinically significant to the nurse?

RELEVANT data from CC:	Rationale:

Medication Application

PMH:	Home Meds:	Pharm. Classification	Expected Outcome:
Diabetes type II	1. Allopurinol 100 mg bid	1.	1.
Hyperlipidemia	2. Colchicine 0.6 mg prn	2.	2.
HTN	3. ASA 81 mg daily	3.	3.
Gout	4. Pioglitazone (Actos) 15 mg daily	4.	4.
	5. Simvastatin 20 mg daily	5.	5.
	6. Metoprolol 25 mg bid	6.	6.
	7. Lisinopril 10 mg daily	7.	7.

One disease process often influences the development of other illnesses. Based on your knowledge of pathophysiology, in your patient (if applicable) which disease likely developed first that then initiated a "domino effect" in her life?
- Circle what PMH problem started **FIRST**
- Underline what PMH problem(s) **FOLLOWED** as domino's

II. Patient Care Begins:
Your Initial VS:
T: 101.8 (o)
P: 110 reg.
R: 24 reg.
BP: 128/82
O2 sats: 98% room air (RA)

What VS data is RELEVANT that must be recognized as clinically significant to the nurse?

RELEVANT VS data:	Rationale:

Your Initial Nursing Assessment:
GENERAL APPEARANCE: Resting comfortably. Appears to be in no apparent distress.
RESPIRATORY: Denies SOB. Breath sounds equal and with good aeration bilaterally.
CARDIAC: Pulses 3+ throughout. No edema in extremities. Heart rate regular-S1S2.
NEUROLOGIC: Alert and oriented x2-is not consistently oriented to date and place.
ABDOMEN/GI: Abdomen soft, non-tender with active bowel sounds. No guarding or point tenderness present.
GENITOURINARY: Admits to dysuria and frequency of urination the past week.
EXTREMITIES/SKIN: Skin is warm and dry-normal for color of skin.

What assessment data is RELAVANT that must be recognized as clinically significant to the nurse?

RELEVANT assessment data:	Rationale:

III. Clinical Reasoning Begins…

1. What is the primary problem that your patient is most likely presenting with?

2. What is the underlying cause /pathophysiology of this concern?

3. What nursing priority will guide your plan of care?

4. What interventions will you initiate based on this priority?

Nursing Interventions	Rationale:	Expected Outcome:

5. What is the most likely/worst possible complication to anticipate?

6. What nursing assessment(s) will you need to initiate to identify this complication if it develops?

Caring and the "Art" of Nursing

7. What is the patient likely experiencing/feeling right now in this situation?

8. What can I do to engage myself with this patient's experience, and show that they matter to me as a person?

Medical Management: Rationale for Treatment & Expected Outcomes

Physician orders:	Rationale:	Expected Outcome:
CXR		
CBC		
BMP		
Lactate		
Place Foley catheter		
UA/UC		
Blood cx x2 sites		
0.9% NS 1000 mL IV bolus		
Acetaminophen 650 mg		
Ceftriaxone 1g IVPB…after blood/urine cultures obtained		

Medication Dosage Calculation

Medication/Dose:	Mechanism of Action:	Volume/timeframe to safely administer:	Nursing Assessment/Considerations:
Ceftriaxone 1g 50 mL IVPB **Normal Range:** (high/low/avg?)		Hourly rate IVPB:	

Radiology Reports:

CXR: No infiltrates or other abnormalities. No changes from last previous

What data above is RELEVANT that must be recognized as clinically significant?

How do these radiology findings relate to primary problem:

Lab Results

CBC	Current	Most Recent
WBC (4.5-11.0)	13.2	8.8
HGB (12-16)	14.4	14.6
PLTS (140-440)	246	140
Neuts. % (42-72)	93	68
Lymphs % (20-44)	5	10

Identify the RELEVANT lab results to this patient and their clinical significance?

Which labs when trended are showing improvement and/or reveal concerning potential complications?

Basic Metabolic Panel	Current	Most Recent
Sodium (135-145)	140	138
Potassium (3.5-5.1)	3.8	3.9
Glucose (65-100)	144	128
Calcium (8.5-10.5)	8.8	8.8
Magnesium (1.8-2.6)	1.8	1.9
Lactate (<2.0)	3.2	n/a
BUN (7-25)	15	14
Creatinine (0.5-1.3)	1.5	1.1

Identify the RELEVANT lab results to this patient and their clinical significance?

Which labs when trended are showing improvement and/or reveal concerning potential complications?

UA	Current
Color (yellow)	Yellow
Clarity (clear)	Cloudy
Sp. Grav (1.002-1.030)	1.008
Protein (neg)	1+
Glucose (neg)	Neg
Ketones (neg)	Neg
Blood (neg)	Neg
Nitrate (neg)	Pos
LET (neg)	Pos
RBC's (0-2)	1
WBC's (0-5)	>100
Bacteria (0-few)	Few
Epithelial (0-few)	Few

Identify the RELEVANT lab results to this patient and their clinical significance?

Which labs when trended are showing improvement and/or reveal concerning potential complications?

PRIORITY LABS: "Lab Planning"

Lab **Lactate** Value **3.2**	Normal value Critical value	Why Relevant???	**Nsg. Assessments/interventions required:**

Lab **Creatinine** Value **1.5**	Normal value Critical value	Why Relevant???	**Nsg. Assessments/interventions required:**

IV. Evaluation:

Evaluate the response of your patient to nursing & medical interventions during your shift. All physician orders have been implemented that are listed under medical management.

Two hours later...
VS:
T: 101.8 (o)
P: 116 reg.
R: 22 reg.
BP: 98/50
O2 sats: 98% RA

What VS data is RELEVANT that must be recognized as clinically significant to the nurse?

RELEVANT VS data:	Rationale:

Nursing Assessment:
GENERAL APPEARANCE: Resting comfortably. Appears to be in no apparent distress.
RESPIRATORY: Denies SOB. Breath sounds equal and with good aeration bilaterally.
CARDIAC: Pulses 3+ throughout. No edema in extremities. Heart rate regular-S1S2.
NEUROLOGIC: Alert and oriented x2-is not consistently oriented to date and place.
ABDOMEN/GI: Abdomen soft, non-tender with active bowel sounds. No guarding or point tenderness present.
GENITOURINARY: Foley catheter draining cloudy urine. 20 mL in the past two hours.
EXTREMITIES/SKIN: Color flushed. Skin is warm and dry centrally, but upper/lower extremities are mottled in appearance and cool to touch.

What assessment data is RELEVANT that must be recognized as clinically significant to the nurse?

RELEVANT assessment data:	Rationale:

1. *Has the status of the patient improved or not as expected to this point?*

2. *What data supports this evaluation assessment?*

3. *Based on your current evaluation, what are your nursing priorities and plan of care?*

4. *What is the rationale for the changes in your patient's status that you have seen to this point?*

Because you have not seen the level of improvement you were expecting in the medical interventions, you decide to update the physician and give the following SBAR:

Situation:

Background:

Assessment:

Recommendation:

The physician agrees with your concerns and decides to repeat the 0.9% NS bolus of 1000 mL. After one hour this has completed and you obtain the following set of VS:
T: 100.6 (o)
P: 92 reg.
R: 20 reg.
BP: 114/84
O2 sats: 98% RA
u/o : 100 mL

1. Has the status of the patient improved or not as expected to this point?

2. What data supports this evaluation assessment?

Your patient who is still in the ED is now being transferred to the intensive care unit (ICU) for close monitoring and assessment. Effective and concise handoffs are essential to excellent care and if not done well can adversely impact the care of this patient. You have done an excellent job to this point, now finish strong and give the following SBAR report to the nurse who will be caring for this patient:

Situation:

Background:

Assessment:

Recommendation

Unfolding Clinical Reasoning Case Study:
Sepsis: ANSWER KEY
I. Data Collection
Chief complaint/History of Present Illness:
Mrs. Kelly is an 82 year old woman who has been feeling more fatigued for the last three days and has had a fever the last twenty-four hours. She reports painful, burning sensation when she urinates as well as frequency of urination the last week. Her daughter became concerned and brought her to the emergency department (ED) when she did not know what day it was. She is mentally alert with no history of confusion.

Personal/Social History:
Mrs. Kelly lives independently in a senior apartment. She is widowed and has two daughters who are active and involved in her life.

*What data is **RELEVANT** that must be recognized as clinically significant to the nurse?*

RELEVANT data from CC:	Rationale:
more fatigued for the last 3 days	*Though a general complaint, when clustered with the following other symptoms, there is a likely PROBLEM! Something of a systemic nature is taking place and it will soon become apparent what this problem is based on the application of your content knowledge!*
fever the last 24 hours	*Fever is reflecting the systemic inflammatory response initiated by the immune system and is there for a reason-to help the body fight off invading micro-organisms by increasing the production of neutrophils; the first responders of the immune system that are macrophages (pacman). The elevated temp also makes it less hospitable for bacteria to thrive and multiply.*
did not know what day it was. She is mentally alert with no history of confusion	*New onset of confusion is always a RED FLAG in the elderly, and when CLUSTERED with the other symptoms, sepsis is becoming the likely cause and the likely primary problem.*
painful, burning sensation when she urinates as well as frequency of urination the last week	*These symptoms are classic with a urinary tract infection (UTI), and with the systemic effects of fatigue, fever and new confusion, the source of this infection is likely uro-sepsis that is common with elderly women.*

Medication Application

PMH:	Home Meds:	Pharm. Classification	Expected Outcome:
Diabetes type II Hyperlipidemia HTN Gout	1. Allopurinol 100 mg bid 2. Colchicine 0.6 mg prn 3. ASA 81 mg daily 4. Pioglitazone (Actos) 15 mg daily 5. Simvastatin 20 mg daily 6. Metoprolol 25 mg bid 7. Lisinopril 10 mg daily	1. anti-gout 2. anti-gout 3. analgesic/NSAID 4. anti-diabetic 5. anti-hyperlipidemic 6. beta blocker 7. ACE Inhibitor	1. Relief of gout sx 2. Same as above 3. Prevention of ACS 4. Control of glucose WNL 5. HDL >35, LDL <100 6. SBP <140 DBP <90 7. Same as above

One disease process often influences the development of other illnesses. Based on your knowledge of pathophysiology, in your patient (if applicable) which disease likely developed first that then initiated a "domino effect" in her life?
- Circle what PMH problem started **FIRST**
  - Diabetes type II-THIS STARTED IT ALL AND SHOULD BE CIRCLED

- Underline what PMH problem(s) **FOLLOWED** as domino's
  - Hyperlipidemia- diabetes increases the progression of atherosclerosis and lipids in the blood
  - HTN-as vascular wall changes are present due to atherosclerosis, HTN then is a natural progression as a result of decreased elasticity of the arterial walls
  - Gout-inconsequential, has no bearing as a domino

II. Patient Care Begins:
Your Initial VS:
T: 101.8 (o)
P: 110 reg.
R: 24 reg.
BP: 128/82
O2 sats: 98% room air (RA)

What VS data is <u>relevant</u> to this patient that must be recognized as clinically significant to the nurse?

RELEVANT VS data:	Rationale:
T: 101.8 (o) P: 110 reg. R: 24	*With an infection of any kind, sepsis is identified by having 2 or more of these criteria of Systemic Inflammatory Response Syndrome (SIRS):* <ul><li>*Temp >100.4 or <96.8*</li><li>*HR >90*</li><li>*RR >20*</li><li>*WBC >12,000 or <4000*</li><li>*Bands >10%*</li></ul> *All three of these VS components meet SIRS criteria, therefore the nurse must recognize that Mrs. Kelly is in sepsis, and is at risk for progression of this syndrome into septic shock. This must be recognized by the nurse and is another clinical RED FLAG!*

Your Initial Nursing Assessment:
GENERAL APPEARANCE: Resting comfortably. Appears to be in no apparent distress.
RESPIRATORY: Denies SOB. Breath sounds equal and with good aeration bilaterally.
CARDIAC: Pulses 3+ throughout. No edema in extremities. Heart rate regular-S1S2.
NEUROLOGIC: Alert and oriented x2-is not consistently oriented to date and place.
ABDOMEN/GI: Abdomen soft, non-tender with active bowel sounds. No guarding or point tenderness present.
GENITOURINARY: Admits to dysuria and frequency of urination the past week.
EXTREMITIES/SKIN: Skin is warm and dry-normal for color of skin.

What assessment data is RELEVANT that must be recognized as clinically significant to the nurse?

It must be noted that in early sepsis it is not uncommon to have a relatively normal physical assessment. Mrs. Kelly does not appear to be that sick. Because early recognition is so crucial to prevent an adverse outcome, the VS are clearly communicating that Mrs. Kelly is already in sepsis/SIRS regardless of how benign her physical assessment may be initially. This application of knowledge provides a heightened vigilance by the nurse that is essential to rescue her, if her status were to change.

RELEVANT assessment data:	Rationale:
GENITOURINARY: Admits to dysuria and frequency of urination the past week.	*This is reflecting the UTI that is the most likely source of sepsis in Mrs. Kelly.*
NEUROLOGIC: Alert and oriented x2- is not consistently oriented to date and place.	*This is reflecting the change in mental status that is commonly seen in sepsis with the elderly.*

III. Clinical Reasoning Begins...

1. **What is the primary problem that your patient is most likely presenting with?**
   Sepsis/urosepsis

2. **What is the underlying cause /pathophysiology of this concern?**

Sepsis Patho...step by step...
This is a general step by step summary. I encourage you to review your nursing textbook or other clinical resources to DEEPEN your knowledge of this content.

1. *Precipitating event...usually bacterial infection.*
2. *Activation of inflammatory response.*
3. *Immune system initiates mediators of inflammatory response w/physiologic consequences (increased temperature...increased HR).*
4. *Increased capillary permeability...fluid leakage...third spacing (which results in TACHYCARDIA as the body begins to compensate for decreased cardiac output (CO) (remember CO=SVxHR!).*
5. *Vasodilation...lowering of BP further and persistent tachycardia.*
6. *Maldistribution of volume (third spacing that will also influence decreasing BP and increasing HR!*
7. *Decreased venous return...lowers PRELOAD as a determinant of CO (this too will lower BP).*
8. *Decreased CO as a result of decreased preload as less venous return comes back to the right side of the heart.*

3. **What nursing priority will guide your plan of care?**
   In this scenario using clinical reasoning and simply stating the nursing priority is reflected in #1. Nursing diagnostic statements also capture the nursing priority and are used in #II, III.

   I. **Obtain all required blood work and blood cultures so that IV antibiotics can be administered ASAP.**

II. Fluid volume deficit...Establish IV access and start IV fluid resuscitation based on physician orders. Recognize that although SBP is not low, establish IV access and start IV fluid resuscitation based on physician orders. Because VS parameters meet 3 criteria for SIRS and has mental status changes, sepsis is present. The nurses APPLICATION OF KNOWLEDGE will facilitate recognition that at a pathophysiologic level, third spacing as well as vasodilation is taking place and Mrs. Kelly will need IV fluids to compensate for this deficit to prevent possible further deterioration.

III. Ineffective tissue perfusion: This nursing priority must be on the nurses radar IF sepsis progresses this priority and resultant nursing interventions will be appropriate.

4. What interventions will you initiate based on this priority?

Nursing Interventions	Rationale:	Expected Outcome:
• *Fluid volume deficit* 1. Establish 2 large bore IV's if possible (18-20g).	1. Has 3 criteria for SIRS. The need for IV fluids and IV antibiotics must be recognized and anticipated by the nurse.	1. IV established
2. Fluid volume resuscitation-ISOTONIC solution-most common 0.9% NS. Anticipate at least one and likely two liters.	2. Early fluid resuscitation is a standard of care in sepsis due to a fluid volume deficit secondary to third spacing influenced by the inflammatory process as well as vasodilation.	2. Cardiac output improves. See parameters below in #3
3. Reassess VS within 15" after each IV bolus is administered..	3. To determine if improvement in fluid volume status is taking place by a **decrease** in HR and **elevation** in SBP. TREND closely to determine trajectory!	3. HR decreases SBP incr. DBP decr.
• *Ineffective tissue perfusion: cardiac, renal, neuro (ANTICIPATE!)* 1. Closely trend and monitor VS parameters of BP, HR, RR as well as color/temp of skin.	1. If condition is improving, HR will decrease and BP increase and RR should be <20. If no systemic inflammatory response present due to sepsis, temp will trend downwards.	1. see above
2. Assess and trend creatinine and urine output closely.	2. To determine adequate renal perfusion.	2. Creatinine trends downward as renal function improves. u/o >30 mL/hr
3. Assess mentation closely for any changes from current baseline.	3. Confusion and worsening change are not uncommon with sepsis/infection and must be carefully trended as a general reflection of overall status.	3. Mentation/confusion improves as sepsis improves.

5. What is the most likely/worst possible complication to anticipate?
Septic shock/Multiple Organ Dysfunction Syndrome (MODS)

6. What nursing assessment(s) will you need to initiate to identify this complication if it develops
*Assess progression/improvement in VS and assessment as it relates to sepsis.
* Frequently monitor and assess the following VS as condition warrants (every 30" to hourly)...temp, HR, BP. Use criteria for SIRS as your clinical red flags-especially BP parameters to note all TRENDS in current status.
*Closely assess confusion and skin for any changes that reflect decreased circulation (cool skin, decreased pulses, pale/diaphoretic).

Caring and the "Art" of Nursing

7. What is the patient likely experiencing/feeling right now in this situation?
I have seen in my own clinical experience that the nurse needs to put themself in the place of the patient to identify what Mrs. Kelly is experiencing in this situation. A starting point to do this practically in practice is to identify the cognitive status of those you care for. Knowing that Mrs. Kelly has a history of being cognitively intact though currently confused to place and time provides a framework to recognize what is needed to support her in this scenario.

In the context of Mrs. Kelly who is critically ill, she is likely aware of this change of status and is fearful, and anxious. I have seen the importance of intentionally supporting both the patient and family by giving them as much information about their current status and explaining the plan of care from both a nursing and medical perspective. KNOWLEDGE is POWER from Mrs. Kelly's perspective, and when the nurse provides this information it will DECREASE anxiety and fear and make a real difference in her well-being.
Even in the context of a patient who is critically ill, when you simply and matter of fact share what you are doing and why, it demonstrates caring and support that is needed.

8. What can I do to engage myself with this patient's experience, and show that they matter to me as a person?
Nurse engagement in any clinical context begins with an attitude and conviction by the nurse that this person matters, and that the nurse does CARE. Practical caring interventions to engage in her experience can be as simple as nurse presence and truly being there for Mrs. Kelly, and using the power of personal touch, and holding her hand as you communicate with her or by not even saying a word, but holding her hand (see chapter one in THINK Like a Nurse!).

It is imperative for the nurse to be sensitive, perceptive, and ENGAGED in order to recognize what Mrs. Kelly needs at any given time. Paying extra attention to NON-VERBAL communication is essential. Though this is a written case study, these principles are derived from my own observations in practice and will readily translate to your practice if they are incorporated to the bedside of every patient you care for!

Medical Management: Rationale for Treatment & Expected Outcomes

Physician orders:	Rationale:	Expected Outcome:
CXR (chest xray)	*Need to rule out any other source of infection such as pneumonia.*	*Negative pathology/WNL*
CBC (complete blood cell count)	*Most relevant labs in this panel are WBC, neutrophils, and bands to gauge severity/degree of*	*Negative pathology/WNL*

	physiologic response to infection.	
BMP (basic metabolic panel)	*Most relevant labs in this panel are K+ and creatinine to gauge renal involvement in sepsis as well as K+ elevation as sepsis progresses because of intracellular leakage of K+ into extracellular space. If renal system takes a hit, K+ will elevate with rising creatinine.*	*Negative pathology/WNL*
Lactate	*Lactate is the closest we have as a lab to identify the presence and progression of sepsis. Lactic acid is the byproduct of anaerobic metabolism and will be elevated if sepsis is progressing.*	*Negative pathology/WNL*
Place Foley catheter	*The benefit of placing a catheter outweighs the risk in this scenario. Knowing that sepsis is present, with the need for close assessment of urine output (u/o), and a sterile urine specimen is needed, this will assist the nurse in identifying concerning trends in renal perfusion.*	*Successfully placed and >30 mL u/o hourly*
UA/UC (urine analysis/urine culture)	*Due to the obvious urinary symptoms this is needed to validate the findings of the UA, but also culture for the specific organism and antibiotic sensitivities. The culture component takes 24-48 hours to confirm, while UA results can be done within an hour or sooner.*	*Negative pathology/WNL*
Blood cultures x2 sites	*Confirms the presence of bacteremia or bacteria in the blood. Culture timeframe and rationale same as for UC.*	*Negative pathology/WNL*
0.9% NS 1000 mL IV bolus	*Early fluid resuscitation is a standard of care in sepsis due to a volume depleted state secondary to third spacing seen in the inflammatory process as well as vasodilation.*	*Improvement in fluid volume deficit that is manifested by decrease in HR and elevation in SBP.*
Acetaminophen 650 mg	*Though a fever can be beneficial in sepsis, most care providers will order to promote patient comfort.*	*Lowering of fever*
Ceftriaxone 1g IVPB…**after blood/urine cultures obtained!**	*As a third generation cephalosporin it binds to the bacterial cell wall membrane, causing cell death.* **Therapeutic Effects:** *Bactericidal action against susceptible bacteria.* **Spectrum:** *Similar to that of second-generation cephalosporins, but activity against staphylococci is less, while activity against gram-negative pathogens is greater.*	*Will not see immediate response in resolving infection, but would expect to see improvement over the next 24 hours*

Medication Dosage Calculation:

| Medication/Dose: Ceftriaxone 1g Normal Range: (high/low/avg?) Avg. | Mechanism of Action: As a third generation cephalosporin it binds to the bacterial cell wall membrane, causing cell death. **Therapeutic Effects:** Bactericidal action against susceptible bacteria. **Spectrum:** Similar to that of second-generation cephalosporins, but activity against staphylococci is less, while activity against gram-negative pathogens is greater | Volume/timeframe to safely administer: 50 ml/30 minutes Hourly rate IVPB: 100 mL/hr on pump | Nursing Assessment/Considerations: Obtain specimens for culture and sensitivity before initiating therapy. First dose may be given before receiving results. Observe patient for signs and symptoms of anaphylaxis (rash, pruritus, laryngeal edema, wheezing). Discontinue the drug and notify health care provider immediately if these symptoms occur. Monitor bowel function. Diarrhea, abdominal cramping, fever, and bloody stools should be reported to health care professional promptly as a sign of pseudomembranous colitis. May begin up to several weeks following cessation of therapy, but not this soon. Keep this on your radar down the road if on antibiotics for several days. |

Radiology Reports:

CXR: No infiltrates or other abnormalities. No changes from last previous

What data above is RELEVANT that must be recognized as clinically significant?
There is no pneumonia as the source of the infection and urine/urosepsis is still the source.

How do these radiology findings relate to primary problem (PP):
They do not relate to primary problem because the CXR is negative.

Lab Results

CBC	Current	Most Recent
WBC (4.5-11.0)	13.2	8.8
HGB (12-16)	14.4	14.6
PLTS (140-440)	246	140
Neuts. % (42-72)	93	68
Lymphs % (20-44)	5	10

Identify the RELEVANT lab results to this patient and their clinical significance?
WBC: 13.2
Body is mounting immune response to underlying infection. WBC elevation is due primarily to the increased production of neutrophils who are the "first responders" of the immune system in response to infection.

Neuts.: 93%
The elevation of neutrophils in response to a bacterial infection begins as early as 6 hours after the initial insult. This % elevation with the increase in overall WBC reveals that the body is responding to a significant invasion of bacteria and has gone systemic! Though >80% neutrophil elevation is a clinical red flag, 90% must be recognized as especially concerning and in the chart health care providers will refer to this significant elevation as a "left shift".

Which labs when trended are showing improvement and/or reveal concerning potential complications?
WBC and neutrophils are both trending upwards at a rate that is a clinical RED FLAG! Sepsis is on the move and is moving in the wrong direction! There is a clear clinical relationship between the increase in neutrophils and the elevation in WBC.

Basic Metabolic Panel	Current	Most Recent
Sodium (135-145)	140	138
Potassium (3.5-5.1)	3.8	3.9
Glucose (65-100)	144	128
Calcium (8.5-10.5)	8.8	8.8
Magnesium (1.8-2.6)	1.8	1.9
Lactate (<2.0)	3.2	n/a
BUN (7-25)	15	14
Creatinine (0.5-1.3)	1.5	1.1

Identify the RELEVANT lab results to this patient and their clinical significance?
Creatinine: 1.5

- *Because there is no history of renal disease this value is extremely significant. Because creatinine is a much more reliable indicator of kidney function/filtration of metabolic waste compared to BUN, it is elevated in Mrs. Kelly because of sepsis/septic shock and lack of perfusion to the kidneys. Regardless of the cause of hypotension, the kidneys will ultimately take a hit. If this lab is elevated it must be trended carefully to see what direction the kidney function is going, especially if volume resuscitation has taken place and BP is restored to WNL.*

Lactate : 3.2

- *This is the most concerning finding that must be watched and trended carefully as its elevation is confirming the possibility of SEPSIS...a systemic infection that can be transported through the blood to the entire body. Lactate elevation reflects anaerobic metabolism that is found in sepsis due to poor perfusion or increased presence of micro-organisms. Remember that the following VS will be impacted: fever, tachycardia with hypotension and each of these must be TRENDED as sepsis progresses. This is the most accurate means to assess and determine current clinical status and what direction Mrs. Kelly will go.*

Which labs when trended are showing improvement and/or reveal concerning potential complications?
Both the lactate and creatinine are progressing in the WRONG direction! These two labs must be continued to be assessed closely as they are rich indicators of what is taking place physiologically. I call this "lab planning" and reflects that a care plan can be derived from the appropriate labs that are most salient to this problem.

UA	Current
Color (yellow)	Yellow
Clarity (clear)	Cloudy
Sp. Grav (1.002-1.030)	1.008
Protein (neg)	1+
Glucose (neg)	Neg
Ketones (neg)	Neg
Blood (neg)	Neg
Nitrate (neg)	Pos
LET (neg)	Pos
RBC's (0-2)	1
WBC's (0-5)	>100
Bacteria (0-few)	Few
Epithelial (0-few)	Few

Identify the RELEVANT lab results to this patient and their clinical significance?
Clarity :Cloudy
- *This finding is usually consistent with infection. The nurse must intentionally assess the clarity of the urine in any pt. who has a catheter to assess for this finding as well!*

WBC's :>100
- *Most clinicians place the highest significance on this specific finding in a UA to determine presence of infection/UTI. Where WBC's are present, they are there for a reason! In this case the level is very high and reflects a positive UTI. Most clinicians will treat if WBC is >5 with symptoms.*

Nitrate: Positive
- *Nitrates are a byproduct of gram negative bacterial metabolism and in this context the most common culprit in women is E. coli. The nurse can make an early assumption if positive that the culprit bacteria causing infection and resultant urosepsis is E. coli.*

LET (leukocyte esterase): Positive
- *Is a gross determinant of the presence of WBC's in the urine. It detects the presence of the enzyme esterase released by leukocytes. You would expect to see this positive if there is a significant presence of micro WBC's in the urine. It is important to put more weight on the micro count of WBC's vs. LET.*

Which labs when trended are showing improvement and/or reveal concerning potential complications?
The labs identified above are all relevant positive and must be continued to be trended to determine progression or improvement in clinical status.

PRIORITY LABS: "Lab Planning"

Lab	Relevance	What caused derangement?	Treatment	Nsg. Assessments/interventions required:
Lactate *Value* **3.2** *Normal range* **<2** *Critical value*	Key indicator for sepsis and anaerobic metabolism. Must be trended carefully for direction of shock state	Lactate is by product of anaerobic metabolism in shock states including sepsis, due to decreased	Correct underlying problem, which in sepsis, is to improve BP, and promote tissue oxygenation	*Assess closely for hypotension with known infection (septic shock). *Assess closely for any change in temperature trend-hypothermia or febrile can both represent sepsis especially in elderly. *Monitor BP and HR closely for concerning trends of increasing HR, and decreasing BP. Remember importance of

>5	when elevated.	oxygenation, anaerobic metabolism increases and therefore any significant elevation in lactate in this patient is a clinical RED FLAG.	through adequate fluid resuscitation and oxygen administration and IV abx.	trending all VS data and assessing what direction these trends are going.

| Lab Creatinine Value 1.5 Normal range 0.5-1.3 mg/dl Critical value >1.5 | Relevance End product of creatine metabolism which is performed in skeletal muscle *Small amount of creatine is converted to creatinine which is then secreted by kidneys. *Amount of creatinine generated proportional to mass of skeletal muscle. | What caused derangement? Lack of perfusion to the kidneys in distributive shock such as sepsis. | Treatment Maximize medical therapy to maximize cardiac output through adequate BP and volume resuscitation. | Nsg. Assessments/interventions required: THINK FLUID BALANCE *Assess I&O closely *Assess for signs of fluid retention/edema as will have some degree of third spacing within hours after receiving IV fluid boluses. *Daily weights |

IV. Evaluation:

Evaluate the response of your patient to nursing and medical interventions during your shift. All physician orders have been implemented that are listed under medical management. Remember to TREND all clinical data from the most recent VS and nursing assessment!

Two hours later...
VS:
T: 101.8 (o)
P: 116 reg.
R: 22 reg.
BP: 98/50
O2 sats: 98% RA

What VS data is <u>relevant</u> to this patient that must be recognized as clinically significant to the nurse?

RELEVANT VS data:	Rationale:
T: 101.8 (o)	*Though the temp has not gone up it has not come down as expected after receiving acetaminophen. Continue to trend temp closely as it reflects the bodies attempt to compensate and fight an acute infection. If it rises further, it could represent a worsening of the underlying infection/sepsis.*
P: 116	*Last HR was 110-after receiving IV fluids, the expected outcome would be to see the HR come DOWN. This has not occurred. This could be due to the underlying fever or progression of sepsis that is causing ongoing vasodilation and third spacing therefore the body is continuing to elevate HR to maintain cardiac output (CO) Remember....CO=SVxHR!*
R: 22	*Remains tachypneic which could reflect underlying hypoxia that is being compensated by tachypnea even though O2 sats are WNL.*
BP: 98/50	*This is where vigilant trending of all VS is essential to all pts-but especially in sepsis. 128/82 was the last BP. Do we have a problem? Though a SBP <90 is a common clinical RED FLAG regarding adequate CV status and a standard for holding most cardiac meds, does this mean we have no reason to be concerned? By TRENDING, in this context a decrease of 30 points in the SBP is too much and must be identified as a clinical RED FLAG!*

Nursing Assessment:
GENERAL APPEARANCE: Resting comfortably. Appears to be in no apparent distress.
RESPIRATORY: Denies SOB. Breath sounds equal and with good aeration bilaterally.
CARDIAC: Pulses 3+ throughout. No edema in extremities. Heart rate regular-S1S2.
NEUROLOGIC: Alert and oriented x2-is not consistently oriented to date and place.
ABDOMEN/GI: Abdomen soft, non-tender with active bowel sounds. No guarding or point tenderness present.
GENITOURINARY: Foley catheter draining cloudy urine. 20 mL u/o in the past two hours.
EXTREMITIES/SKIN: Color flushed. Skin is warm and dry centrally, but upper/lower extremities are mottled in appearance and cool to touch.

What assessment data is RELEVANT that must be recognized as clinically significant to the nurse?

RELEVANT assessment data:	Rationale:
EXTREMITIES/SKIN: Color flushed. Skin is warm and dry centrally, but upper/lower extremities are mottled in appearance and cool to touch.	*When assessment findings are TRENDED, what has changed from last assessment is that upper/lower extremities are now cool to the touch. As sepsis progresses circulation is shunted centrally due to peripheral vasoconstriction. This makes this assessment finding significant and warrants close assessment for possible progression of sepsis to septic shock!* *This is the significance of mottled extremities as well. This is reflecting impaired circulation and when clustered with the coolness of extremities is a clinical RED FLAG that must be recognized by the nurse!*
GENITOURINARY: Foley catheter	*Cloudy urine is expected since we know that she has a positive UTI. The*

draining cloudy urine. 20 mL in the past two hours.	*amount must be noted as TOO LOW! Remember that 30 mL u/o is a clinical standard for most adult patients, and when decreased here, is likely reflecting worsening sepsis with shunting of blood from the kidneys to the core.*

1. Has the status of the patient improved or not as expected to this point?
Not as expected. The assessment reveals that the expected outcomes of medical management to this point have not been met.

2. What data supports this evaluation assessment?
Upper/lower extremities are cool to touch as well as mottled.
u/o is declining and has had only 20 mL in the past two hours.

3. Based on your current evaluation, what are your nursing priorities and plan of care?
Nursing Priorities:
*Initiate SBAR to update the physician on current status and would strongly recommend the need for at least 1 additional liter of NS and assess response in lowering of HR and improving BP
*Assess progression/improvement in VS (HR-BP-temp) and assessment especially u/o as it relates to sepsis.
* If VS parameters continue to deteriorate, contact physician to administer additional fluids or contact Rapid Response Team if available to facilitate transfer to ICU.

Plan of Care:
* Frequently monitor and assess the following VS as condition warrants (in this pt on the floor hourly VS would be reasonable)....temp, HR, BP.
*closely assess confusion and skin for any changes as well as hourly u/o.

4. What is the rationale for the changes in your patient's status that you have seen to this point?
As sepsis progresses circulation is shunted centrally due to peripheral vasoconstriction. This makes this assessment findings of decreased u/o as well as mottled extremities significant and warrants close assessment for possible progression of sepsis to septic shock

Because you have not seen the level of improvement you were expecting in the medical interventions, you rightly decide to update the physician and give the following SBAR:
Because this SBAR is to the ED physician who knows the patient, it is not necessary to give as much information in the SB of the SBAR. This principle is also true for those patients you will give an SBAR to who know the patient or are the primary care provider. Be flexible and modify the SBAR as needed depending on the knowledge of the one who is receiving the SBAR!

Situation:
- *82 year old woman with positive UTI and likely urosepsis*

Background:
- *Known to physician. Do not need to restate.*

Assessment:
After receiving 1 liter of 0.9% NS have not seen significant improvement in VS. This is what was obtained after first liter of NS:
- T: 101.8 (o)
- P: 116 reg.
- R: 22 reg.
- BP: 98/50

Recommendation:
- Needs additional 1 liter of NS bolus. Will closely assess response.

The physician agrees with your concerns and decides to repeat the 0.9% NS bolus of 1000 mL. After one hour this has completed and you obtain the following set of VS:

T: 100.6 (o)
P: 92 reg.
R: 20 reg.
BP: 114/84
O2 sats: 98% RA
u/o : 100 mL

1. Has the status of the patient improved or not as expected to this point?
Absolutely! It appears that this additional bolus has stabilized patient and replaced needed volume.

2. What data supports this evaluation assessment?

T: 100.6 (o)
- *Minimal improvement noted, but is TRENDING in the right direction!*

P: 92
- *HR has decreased from 116 to 92-a significant improvement that reflects that volume status at this time is improving. The clinical relationship of temperature decrease and HR decrease must also be recognized by the nurse.*

R: 20
- *Slight decrease from 22 to 20, though not a large decrease is TRENDING in the right direction!*

BP: 114/84
- *The increase in SBP and decrease in DBP must be noted as a reflection of improvement in fluid volume status (widened pulse pressure)!*

Your patient who is still in the ED is now being transferred to the intensive care unit (ICU) for close monitoring and assessment. Effective and concise handoffs are essential to excellent care and if not done well can adversely impact the care of this patient. You have done an excellent job to this point, now finish strong and give the following SBAR report to the nurse who will be caring for this patient:

SBAR's need to be kept as concise as possible when giving report to the nurse or physician. Make it a priority to emphasize clinical data that is RELEVANT. This is what I would emphasize in my SBAR to the receiving nurse:

Situation:
- *Mrs. Kelly is an 82 year old woman who has been feeling more fatigued for the last 3 days and has had a fever the last 24 hours. She reports painful, burning sensation when she urinates as well as frequency of urination the last week. Her daughter became concerned and brought her to the emergency department (ED) when she did not know what day it was. She is mentally alert with no history of confusion*

Background:
- *PMH of diabetes type II and HTN*

Assessment:
Initial VS:
T: 101.8 (o)
P: 110 reg.
R: 24 reg.
BP: 128/82
O2 sats: 98% room air (RA)

- *Initial assessment WNL with exception of new confusion to date and place.*
- *Foley catheter placed without incident.*
- *Admitting labs:*
    - *WBC: 13.2*
    - *Neutrophils: 93%*
    - *UA: positive for UTI with >100 WBC's per micro*
    - *Creatinine 1.5*
    - *Lactate 3.2*
- *Received a total of two liters of NS bolus.*
- *Ceftriaxone 1 g IVPB given.*
- *BP dropped to 98/50 after first liter of NS, but has since rebounded to 114/84 after the second bolus. HR has improved and decreased from 110 to 92 currently.*
- *Temperature decreased to 100.6 (o)*
- *u/o was initially only 20 mL first two hours in ED, but has since had 100 mL in the past hour.*

Recommendation
- *Is currently stable, but at risk for progression of sepsis. Continue to monitor u/o and VS closely.*

Chapter 6: Clinical Pearls

I want to identify some "clinical pearls" that I have found to be most relevant to my nursing practice in the acute care setting. Though this list is not exhaustive, you can dovetail these pearls with what your program taught you and your own clinical setting to further prepare you for professional practice!

Head to Toe Nursing Assessment

Your priority in practice is to identify SUBTLE changes EARLY that are clinically significant. This requires thoroughness and attention to detail. Though it should be obvious, do not forget the importance of TOUCHING your patient. I recently assisted a nurse who was concerned about her patient who was not doing so well. He was pale, but not diaphoretic. When I intentionally touched his forehead he was ice cold! This simple assessment spoke volumes and when I clustered this assessment finding with the need to recheck his BP and it was now 68/30, I knew I had a problem and a patient who needed to be rescued! This is why there is no such thing as a ROUTINE assessment or set of vital signs!

Vital Signs

- Do not use the heart rate found on the blood pressure machine or oximeter as you collect VS. These are notoriously inaccurate and are influenced by a number of variables. Therefore, spend the extra fifteen to thirty seconds and palpate a radial pulse to ensure accuracy of your clinical data. Nothing replaces human validation!
- You also need to palpate the pulse to validate the accuracy of every oximeter reading you collect in practice. In order for the oximeter reading to be believable, the heart rate on the oximeter must be within 4-8 beats of what you just palpated. If the heart rates do not correlate, the oximeter reading is not reliable. This is an especially important assessment validation to do whenever the oximeter reading is <90%. This is the gold standard to ensure the accuracy of your oximeter reading!
- Be sure that you use the right size BP cuff! Though this is going back to fundamentals, I routinely find cuffs that are clearly too large or too small in practice on my patient. If the cuff is too large for a patient, the numbers will skew to being lower than actual, and if too small, it will skew higher than actual.
- If your patient has a PICC in the upper arm or is obese with thick upper arms, do not hesitate to use the lower forearm with a smaller cuff instead. As long as the cuff is the correct size and the

pulse arrow is on top of the radial pulse, I have found this to be accurate with minimal difference compared to the traditional upper arm location.

Respiratory
- Breath sounds
    - Posterior auscultation is always preferred because there is less body tissue and adventitious breath sounds can readily be identified if present. Remember the right lower lobe is easier to auscultate from the back.
    - ALWAYS start at the top and compare one lobe laterally to the opposite side listening carefully for not only the presence of abnormal sounds but also the quality of the aeration. If pneumonia or pleural effusion is present, the only assessment finding could be diminished aeration and this is clinically significant.
    - Auscultate four levels of the lung fields: upper, mid, lower, and lower lateral.
    - ALWAYS listen very carefully as you approach the mid/lower lobes because this is where most adventitious sounds start, especially crackles because of gravity.
    - If wheezing is present, be sure to note if they are on inspiration or expiration. Expiratory wheezes are most common, but if inspiratory wheezing is present, can reflect a greater degree of bronchoconstriction and is clinically significant.
    - If crackles are present, the degree of coarseness correlates with the amount of fluid in the alveoli. For example, fine crackles represent small amount of fluid or even atelectasis while coarse crackles are reflecting more fluid in the alveoli.

- Rhythm/character
    - If respiratory distress is present for any reason, in addition to noting the rate, be sure to also determine if any retractions are present. Intercostal retractions are most common with adults and children.
    - With infants, any retractions if present are a clinical RED FLAG! Intercostal retractions typically represent mild to moderate distress, but if sternal retractions are present this represents severe distress.

Cardiac
- General
    - Diaphoresis is ALWAYS clinically significant and reflects sympathetic nervous system stimulation. The nurse must step back and ask WHY? What is most likely causing this based on their story and most likely/worst possible complication.
    - Orthostatic BP's: Positive ortho's...remember the number **20**. INCREASE of HR >20 or DECREASE in systolic blood pressure (SBP) >20 represent a positive orthostatic BP. If mild-moderate volume depletion, will typically see HR increase with no change in SBP. If both the HR INCREASES and SBP DECREASES, then the fluid volume deficit is much more pronounced in severity and is a clinical RED FLAG!
    - Potassium is the electrolyte that is most rapidly depleted during diuresis with any loop diuretic such as furosemide (Lasix). Therefore, if there has been a vigorous diuresis (>1000 mL/shift) and potassium was low normal, it is most likely now below normal and you will need to recheck and assess telemetry closely for increased frequency of premature ventricular contractions (PVC's) or other signs and symptoms of hypokalemia.
    - Remember that a patient cannot absorb potassium if the magnesium is not normal. So check both Mg+ and K+ and replace the magnesium first unless the potassium is too low, then you may need a second IV line to start both simultaneously.

- Heart sounds
    - You MUST know the location and physiologic landmarks of the four valves: aortic, pulmonic, tricuspid, and mitral. This is relevant because many of your patients will have valvular disease or have had valve surgery and you must know the location of that valve, listening carefully for any murmurs or adventitious sounds. If your patient has aortic stenosis, where will you auscultate?
    - To help visualize the first two auscultation landmarks, remember your favorite prerequisite A&P (anatomy and physiology)!
        - ✓ The **A**ortic valve is second intercostal to the RIGHT of the sternum. The manubrium is the "bump" on the top end of the sternum that is your landmark for the second intercostal space.
        - ✓ The **P**ulmonic valve is also second intercostal across the sternum on the LEFT side.

- - For the last two landmarks remember TM, an abbreviation for tympanic membrane.
    - ✓ The **T**ricuspid valve is fourth to fifth intercostal on the LEFT side of the sternum. This level is also consistent with the nipple line of men, and is the lower third of the sternum to visualize for women.
    - ✓ The **M**itral valve is the same intercostal level, just slide the stethoscope over to LEFT mid-clavicular. On a male this is typically right at the left nipple. This is also the location for an apical pulse.
  - To be considerate of women, when auscultating the tricuspid and mitral valves which are over the left breast, I will auscultate ABOVE the breast and typically be closer to the fourth intercostal landmark so I am not as intrusive by auscultating BELOW the breast.
  - When auscultating heart sounds, S1S2 represents a distinct "lub-dub." Most murmurs are systolic and will be heard at the first heart sound or "lub" and sound like this…"whooosh-dub."
  - In addition to identifying S1S2, the nurse must also assess for the presence of an additional heart sound or gallop.
    - ✓ S3 is a splitting gallop of the second heart sound. Upon auscultation, this additional gallop will sound just like the state: "Ken-tuck-y."
    - ✓ S4 is a splitting gallop of the first heart sound. Upon auscultation, this additional gallop will sound just like the state: "Ten-ness-ee."

- Strength/regularity of peripheral pulses
  - ALWAYS assess both right and left extremity pulses at the same time to determine true equality and any subtle changes that may be clinically significant.
  - Closely assess the regularity of pulses not just the rate. If irregular, most common arrhythmia is atrial fibrillation and must be considered, especially if rate >100.

- Cap refill
  - Though textbook norm is <3 seconds, most patients even with vascular disease are brisk and <1 second. I am concerned if cap refill is equal or >2 seconds.
  - If your patient has fungal toenails and are unable to visualize the color of the toenail, blanch the tip of the toe instead.

- Color/temperature extremities
    - ALWAYS assess warmth/coolness of both right and left extremities at the same time to determine true equality and any subtle changes that may be clinically significant.

- Telemetry rhythm (if applicable)
    - Regularly check monitor throughout shift. Rhythm changes occur quickly and will not always alarm. Atrial fibrillation is the most common arrhythmia and most likely to present clinically.
    - Increased frequency of premature atrial contractions (PAC's) represents increased atrial irritability and can be an early warning that atrial fibrillation is just around the corner.
    - Increased PVC's and especially multi-focal PVC's represent ventricular irritability and runs of V-tach may be just around the corner.
    - Remember the relationship of potassium and magnesium to cardiac electrical conduction. Therefore, if these electrolytes are low, you will likely see increased electrical irritability that will be recognized as frequent PVC's, V-tach, or atrial fibrillation.

- Edema…location/degree
    - Be sure to differentiate pitting vs. non-pitting edema in the lower extremities by gently but firmly placing your fingertips for 2-3 seconds in the tissue and then assess the depth of the "pit." Remember that edema or fluid in the tissues may also be in the lungs!
    - Systematically assess for not only the depth of pitting edema but also how far up the legs it is present. Start at the feet and work your way up until there is clearly no "pit" present. In severe heart failure you can see pitting edema into the thighs.
    - Though some nursing textbooks quantify the depth of edema in 2mm increments (1+ is 2mm) the definition at your facility may be different. I have seen the most common scale is graded by ¼ inch increments instead. So 1+ pitting edema would be documented if the "pit" was appx. ¼ inch.

Neuro
- a/o x4 (person-place-time-situation)

- If your patient is on narcotics, establish the baseline orientation EARLY, so if there are any subtle changes later in your shift, you will know they are new and may be clinically significant.

- Level of consciousness (LOC)
    - If your patient is on narcotics, establish the baseline LOC early, so if there are any subtle changes later in your shift, you will know they are new and may be clinically significant.
    - Remember that with narcotic over sedation, change in LOC or orientation are the EARLY signs of CNS depression and a decreased respiratory rate (<10) is a LATE finding.

GI

- Tenderness w/palpation
    - Palpate 1-2 inches deep systematically in each quadrant to determine if tenderness is present. I find that most students feel they will harm their patient and tend to do shallow palpation of <1 inch.
    - Closely assess for soft/firmness of abdomen when palpated. A firm abdomen can reflect ileus or constipation and must be noted.

- Bowel sounds/flatus/Last bowel movement (LBM)
    - Pay close attention to the LBM, especially if your patient is post-op. This can get easily missed and must be noted as this is clinically significant if there has been no BM in the last two to three days. Check the flow sheet to validate and always ask the patient if they can recall LBM if they are reliable.

- NG placement
    - If placing a Salem® sump tube for gastric decompression, run warm water over the entire tube for at least thirty seconds to soften the relatively stiff plastic tubing which will facilitate correct placement.
    - The most painful and difficult aspect of NG placement is getting the tube into the posterior pharynx. When inserting the tube into the naris, point the tube once in the naris to the inner canthus of the opposite eye. This follows the typical anatomic

structure of the nose and septum. You can also gently curve the tube prior to insertion by gently winding it around your finger.
- Always have a second person available to assist with placement for two reasons. First, you need them to assist with sips of water as you guide the tube from the posterior pharynx to the esophagus. Second, I have had unexpected levels of anxiety and agitation from non-confused patients who begin to actively fight you as you attempt to place the tube. Having the second person hold the hands and provide additional reassurance will make placement possible.

GU

- Urine amount/color/clarity
    - ALWAYS assess the color/clarity of urine in the clear tubing of the catheter and continue to assess during the shift with each assessment. It is not uncommon to have the urine be initially clear and then change to cloudy or have sediment present. This could reflect a new UTI and is clinically significant.

- Foley
    - ALWAYS make sure that the catheter has some type of securement device; this is the best practice to prevent needless trauma and decrease incidence of UTI.

Skin

- Color/temperature
    - Central coolness when touching the forehead can be clinically significant and must be noted. When sepsis is early, the extremities will likely be cool, but as it progresses the core as well as the extremities will be cool/cold.

- Skin integrity
    - Most common pressure point to carefully assess is the coccyx. Remember the significance of redness and if present determine if blanchable or not. If redness is slow to return (>2 seconds) this is a clinical RED FLAG that reflects tissue is close to breaking down. Gray or ashen color means ischemia to the area so make sure you get the patient off their coccyx by repositioning them.

- Mucous membranes
    - To quickly and easily identify dehydration with adults or pediatrics, look first at the lips. Unusual dryness is common with mild dehydration.
    - Have patient open their mouth and assess the mouth and tongue for saliva. It should appear moist and shiny. If it is dry or tacky this is a progression of dehydration and is likely mild to moderate in severity depending on the story. I find this much easier and practical than assessing for "tenting" of skin, though they can both be done together.

Miscellaneous
- Priority setting with multiple patients
    - This is going to be one of the biggest challenges as a new nurse. Instead of one to two patients that is typical in nursing education clinical assignments, you will be responsible for three to seven patients in acute care depending on the shift and the floor. In transitional care units (TCU) or long-term care (LTC) you can easily double or triple these numbers.
    - In acute care, the following principles have proved helpful to guide me when I have multiple patients to determine who should be seen FIRST.
        - ✓ *How old is the patient?*
            - The older the patient, the higher risk they are. Therefore if all considerations are equal, see the oldest patient FIRST.
        - ✓ *When were they admitted?*
            - The more recent the admission day, the potential for being a higher acuity and risk for a change of status is present. Therefore if all considerations are equal, see the most recent admitted patient FIRST.
        - ✓ *When did they have surgery?*
            - The more recent the day of surgery, the potential for being a higher acuity and risk for a change of status is present. Therefore if all considerations are equal, see the most recent surgical patient FIRST.

- ✓ *How many body systems are involved?*
  - Chronic renal failure patients are an excellent example of patients who typically have multiple body system derangements because of the systemic metabolic changes influenced by renal disease. If medical complexity is present, they should be seen FIRST.

- ✓ *Any clinical RED FLAGS that are recognized from the chart or from nurse report.*

- Labeling syringes with IV medications
  - It is essential to label all syringes that you have drawn up and will take into the patient's room to administer. One quick and easy way to do this is to take a piece of tape and attach the neck of the IV bottle to the cap of the needle on the syringe. This accomplishes two things: labels syringe, and by not taping the body of the bottle you can easily scan the medication if your institution utilizes bedside scanning.

Emotional Support/Needs

Though this was covered in chapter 1, I want to highlight some important points that are worth repeating!

- Put yourself in the shoes of your patient; it will go a long way to promote caring behaviors and nurse engagement.
- Do not be afraid to engage and experience at a healthy level your patient's experience. This is a privilege, not a burden!
- Avoid the assumptions that the prior nurse's experience with the patient will be your own. I have received numerous "loaded reports" of how bad my day is going to be because the patient is a very difficult person. Instead of assuming this will be your experience, wipe your mental slate clean, stay positive and respectful. Many times the real issue is that there was a personality conflict, NOT a difficult patient.
- Recognize the power of your caring presence. Just being there and available to your patient demonstrates caring. Conveying this availability by simply stating, "Here is the call light. *I am available* to you whenever you need me," can powerfully communicate caring.

These pearls on assessment will help you to recognize EARLY TRENDS of a changing status and the need to rescue your patient if "Jason" is getting closer. Though there are a number of ways that the status of your patient can change, remember that the "fight or flight" physiologic responses of the sympathetic nervous system are universal when "Jason" is near. Therefore, pale moist skin, diaphoresis, tachycardia, tachypnea, and restlessness/anxiety that cannot be readily explained or is a recent change are ALWAYS clinically significant. Situate these and other pearls into your practice and you will be that nurse who makes a difference by rescuing and protecting your patients from "Jason" before it is too late!

Tools of the Trade
- ALWAYS have a pocket full of alcohol wipes before you start your clinical shift. You will use them for numerous purposes such as preparing the skin for any injections and cleansing the hub of IV tubing before administering medications.
- I have found that having a scissors, forceps and medical tape are essential tools of the trade. You can carry them with you at all times by taking a forceps, then thread the tip through your roll of tape and attach the forceps to the side of your pants at the belt loop level. Then take a bandage scissors and place in the center of the tape hole. You then have all three pieces of equipment in one place and all together at your side when you need them!
- Purchase a QUALITY stethoscope. Quality does matter and you will notice the difference. If you got through nursing school with an inexpensive model because of your budget, it is now time to splurge or, better yet, they make a perfect graduation gift! A friend of mine told me that it is not the cost of the stethoscope that matters; it is **what is between the ears** of the person using it! Though there is no substitute for a thinking nurse, for less than $100 I recommend the following models that I have used in practice:

    o ADC Adscope 600 Platinum Edition Ultimate Acoustic Cardiology
      ✓ This is my favorite and is pictured on the cover of this book! It has the best acoustics, but is closer to $85.
      ✓ The ADC is half the price of a comparable Littman cardiology stethoscope but has no appreciable difference in quality or acoustics.

- Littman II SE
  - ✓ This is an all-around workhorse and can be used in all clinical areas. It has slightly less quality in acoustics, but the difference is negligible. Priced at $60.

Additional Resources:

- Flashcards: *Mosby's Assessment Memory NoteCards: Visual, Mnemonic, and Memory Aids for Nurses,* 2nd edition by JoAnn Zerwekh & Tom Gaglione

Chapter 7: Clinical Wisdom from Nurses in Practice

In closing, I have captured the clinical wisdom and encouragement from experienced nurses, some old and some new, whom I respect and have been blessed to work with in clinical practice. Their insights have been tested, tried, and refined through their clinical experience. If you note any recurrent themes of wisdom from these responses, recognize that this point is especially relevant for you to consider!

- *"Pay attention to the PATIENT because it is so easy to miss something. I recently had a patient who was lethargic and I was not clear as to why. By asking myself "WHY IS THIS?" I had an ABG done and the CO_2 was >100; he needed to be intubated. Also pay attention to the LITTLE THINGS. Check IV tubing and all connections on your patient to prevent problems before they start. Some days you will make a mistake and feel like quitting. It is easy to think it would be better somewhere else, but you need to have the courage to keep coming back."*
    Pam-RN, 30 years/ICU

- *"Know your medications! The time-action-profile found in nursing drug handbooks is essential to know so you know when to follow up and assess the response to what you gave to see if it is working. As a newer nurse, identify the best and most approachable nurses on your floor so they can be a real world resource as well as an example to model your nursing practice by."*
    Andrew-RN, 1 year/med-surg

- *"Never be afraid to ask questions. You will get yourself into trouble if you don't, and you will learn a lot more if you do!"*   Melissa-RN, 3 years/ICU

- *"Lean heavily on experienced nurses; not those who eat their young, but those that are safe to ask questions."*   Mike-RN, 16 years/ICU

- *"Have a willingness to put your ego aside and do not feel that you have to prove yourself and show that you know it all. Remain teachable."*   Eric-RN, 8 years ED/ICU

- *"Give it a year to become comfortable in practice. I was ready to quit after six months because I was unsure of myself in practice. I was worried that I was going to harm my patients. Also do *not be afraid to ask questions! I am always concerned about a new nurse who appears to know it all."*

                                                                  Brant-RN, 10 years/ICU

- *"Time management. Be ready to multitask with at least 3-4 patients. Focus on patient care, NOT on charting."*   Jay-RN, 3 months/ED

- *"Treat your patients like you would want your family members to be treated."*   Jill-RN, 20 years/ED

- *"Be prepared to make mistakes because you are still human."*   Darcy-RN, 10 years/ED

- *"Forgive yourself when you make mistakes or when you do not know what you think you should know."*   Tracy-RN, 22 years/ED

- *"You don't know what you don't know. The only dumb question is the one not asked."*   Mandy-RN, 6 years/ED

- *"Ask questions. Expect to flounder the first six months. Treat your patients like family members."*   Rana-RN, 9 years/ED

- *"Trust your gut. You know more than you think you do. Give yourself credit for what you already know."*   Rachel-RN 5 years/Float Pool

- *"Give yourself at least one year to get comfortable in practice. Learn to set priorities as this is the foundation to practice. Know what you can change and what you cannot. Also ask, ask, ask! There is so much that you don't know, that you don't even know it."*   Gayle-RN, 40 years/Float Pool

- *"Accept your limitations. Know when to ask for help."*   Melina-RN, 17 years/Float Pool

- *"A good nurse is always willing to ask questions even if it makes them look stupid. It is better to be willing to appear stupid than be dangerous to your patients."*

                                                                     David-RN, 17 years/Float Pool

- *"Don't be afraid to step back from a stressful situation and take a deep breath when you are feeling overwhelmed. Get your priorities straight and do not miss the big picture."*
  Justin-RN, 1 year/ED

- *"Time management is key. Know who your priority is and see those patients first because things can change so quickly."* Michelle-RN, 5 years/Float Pool

- *"You will not spend hours obsessing over care plans as you do in nursing school. In practice you need to identify what is your care priority and what will you do to advance the plan of care. It is that simple."* Kate-RN, 10 years/Float Pool

- *"Look at the BIG PICTURE with every patient. Do not focus on the tasks, but look at the patient and see how they look and how they are doing."* Becky, 25 years/med-surg

- *"Watch your patient closely and stay in tune with your patient. Then you will be able to identify when something changes. Though you may not be able to identify specifically what you are assessing, you will know that it is different from their baseline and will recognize the need to do something."* Alice-RN, 20 years/ICU

- *"Use your eyes, ears and really look and listen to your patient. Be thorough and be vigilant. Remember that there is no such thing as a routine assessment!"*
  Carrie-RN, 6 years/Float Pool

- *"Trust your intuition, even if the doctor says not to worry about it! If you sense that something is wrong in your gut, don't ignore it because it is almost always right."*
  Marcia-RN, 7 years/PACU

- *"It's OK to be scared. It's OK to ask questions. It's OK to delegate to give some of your work away. Recognize your limitations knowing that you can't do it all."*
  Shawn-RN, 15 years/Float Pool

- *"Know who your resources are every shift such as your charge nurse and colleagues that you trust. To effectively communicate with the physician when you call know three things: what is your concern, what is your assessment data to validate the concern, and know what you want! (Remember the R of SBAR?) If the physician becomes upset or short with you, don't let it affect* you. Be a turtle and let it roll off your back knowing that you are advocating for your patient."

Louellen-RN, 27 years/Float Pool

- *"Learn to be kind. Not only for your patients but for yourself. Be true to yourself but hold back the biting words. Think before you speak then follow your gut."*

Kari-RN, 30 years, RRT

- *"Instead of complaining about what a horrible day it is or will be because of... Embrace adversity and the daily challenges that are not uncommon in clinical practice. If you see adversity as a challenge to OVERCOME instead of something to ENDURE, you will thrive instead of merely surviving!"*

Keith-RN, 30 years/Float Pool

- *"Be honest in all interactions with patients, family members, colleagues, and providers. Always look at your patient. Pay attention to your patient and what they are saying. Hold your nursing ethics close to your heart and your clinical practice!"*

Georgia-RN, 29 years, Surgery Nurse

Appendix A

Skeletons in the Closet: Nurse-to-Nurse Bullying and Incivility

Every house has closets and some have a few skeletons in those closets. Unfortunately, the living house of professional practice is no different and has two skeletons that must be clearly identified so that they do not rob you of the life and passion you desire to bring into your practice. The first skeleton represents the endemic problem of unprofessional, disrespectful behaviors in nursing that go by a multitude of names: incivility, lateral violence, horizontal hostility, and workplace bullying. The other skeleton, detailed in appendix B, is gender bias toward men in nursing that began with Nightingale and other early nurse leaders at the beginning of the modern era and still lingers in various forms today.

Beware of Bullies

Bullying did not only happen on the playground when you were a child, but has been found to be present in all levels of primary education, nursing education, personal relationships, and in the workplace today (1). In nursing, it is commonly acknowledged and understood that "nurses eat their young," which unintentionally normalizes this destructive behavior. Bullying is defined by a **consistent pattern** of inappropriate abusive/aggressive behavior toward another colleague that is designed to intimidate, control, diminish, or devalue another (2). Incivility "is defined as rude or disruptive behaviors that often result in psychological or physiological distress for the people involved and, if left unaddressed, may progress into threatening situations" (3). How incivility and bullying impact another human being is what matters most. It is an assault on human dignity and self-worth, and the effects can be devastating, debilitating, and enduring (4).

Bullying Behaviors: in the Clinical Setting

The most common overt bullying behaviors include patterns of faultfinding, intimidation, gossip, put downs, and nonverbal innuendo such as raising eyebrows or sighing. More subtle bullying behaviors include isolation, exclusion, ignoring/refusing to help, and unfair assignments (2). Other categories of bullying behavior include the resentful nurse who holds grudges and encourages others to join in as well as the cliquish nurse who intentionally excludes others from their "group" (5). Other specific examples from the literature most commonly seen include:

- Having information withheld so it affects your performance
- Being ordered to do work below your level of competence
- Having your views and opinions ignored

- Being personally ignored or excluded
- Excessive monitoring of your work
- Persistent criticism of your work and effort
- Having insulting/offensive remarks made about you
- Hints from others that you should quit your job
- Repeated reminders of your errors and mistakes
- Having false allegations or accusations made against you (6)

I have experienced some of these behaviors personally in the clinical setting. The most common examples of incivility consisted of being marginalized and isolated on a unit by nurses who were unwilling to help. If I asked for help they would sigh and make it clear that I was asking too much. During report, some nurses appeared disinterested, distracted, and asked numerous questions not even relevant to the patient's priority problem. When I didn't have this non-essential information, the nurse would look at me in a demeaning manner.

I have seen newer nurses break down and begin to cry when asked how they were doing as a new nurse on the unit. One nurse described the need to prove herself, feeling belittled if she asked a question because the nurse would respond, *"You don't know that?"* in a demeaning tone of voice. Routinely new nurses overheard gossip about them or others and did not feel safe asking questions of certain nurses.

Root Causes

One way to understand incivility is to recognize that bullying is RELATIONAL AGGRESSION, which is a feminine form of aggressive behavior. Though men are also fully capable of bullying behaviors, men most often resort to physical aggression with conflict. But because women comprise the majority of nurses, bullying as relational aggression is endemic and situated throughout the nursing profession (5). Another perspective to consider is that bullying is a learned behavior that is accepted as "normal" and expected (7). Just as relational aggression among young women is normalized in adolescence through such vernacular as "mean girls," this accepted norm then becomes a self-fulfilling prophecy of what to expect in a profession where women are the majority. This may explain in part why there is an acceptance or tolerance of bullying today. This pattern then continues unchallenged because nurses do not challenge the status quo but are willing to put up with it to avoid conflict at all costs (7).

Though bullying typically involves student peers or colleagues in the profession; it is also present when there is an unequal power relationship. In academia this can be typified by the dean, department chair, or senior faculty who bullies a new faculty member or when faculty members bully students. In the workplace, this unequal power relationship occurs when charge nurses and nurse managers bully other staff nurses or aides.

Consequences

The consequences of a hostile work environment are devastating, creating feelings of inadequacy in a new nurse. Bullying is like putting gas on the fire of inadequacy, and feelings of failure, decreased self-esteem, self-doubt, anger, depression, burnout, and even post-traumatic stress disorder (PTSD) are common (2). This then leads to decreased morale, low job satisfaction, increased absenteeism, and ultimately leaving the unit or even nursing entirely (8). Thirty percent of new nurses leave their first job after the first year when bullying is personally experienced (6).

Does this toxic environment impact patient care? Absolutely! The Joint Commission has taken the position that bullying is a safety issue and has issued a standard to that effect. It has been shown that a unit that has a prevalence of bullying behaviors can lead to increased medical errors, adverse patient outcomes, and lower rates of nurse retention. By creating an environment that does not make it safe to ask questions, incivility poses a serious threat to patient safety and overall quality of care (9).

Though workplace bullying occurs in all work settings, healthcare occupations have the highest rates of bullying (6). Surveys have shown that 93 percent of nurses have witnessed bullying and 85 percent reported that they were victims of bullying (10). Sixty-four percent of nurses cited this as the primary reason for leaving their current job (11). New nurses as well as men in nursing (5), are more likely to experience incivility most often from other more experienced or senior nurses (12).

Be a Team Player!

Teamwork and collaboration is a relevant QSEN competency to clinical practice that must be embraced by the nurse in practice as an antidote to bullying in the workplace. Teamwork and collaboration is defined as the nurse who "functions effectively within nursing and interprofessional teams, fostering open communication, mutual respect, and shared decision making to achieve quality patient care (13). The attitudes needed in order to be a true team player include:

- VALUING the perspective and expertise of ALL health team members
- RESPECT the centrality of the patient/family as core members of any healthcare team
- RESPECT the unique attributes that members bring to a team, including variations in professional orientations and accountabilities
- APPRECIATE importance of all professional collaboration
- VALUE TEAMWORK and the relationships upon which it is based

- VALUE different styles of communication used by patients, families and health care providers
- CONTRIBUTE to resolution of conflict and disagreement (13)

Though these QSEN attitudes are inherently practical, they are not enough! The following BEHAVIOURS as a nurse must also be actively integrated and possessed:
- Act with integrity, consistency, and respect for differing views
- Demonstrate awareness of one's strengths and limitations as a team member
- Initiate requests for help when appropriate to the situation
- Function competently within one's scope of practice as a member of the healthcare team
- Communicate with team members, adapting one's style of communicating to needs of the team and situation
- Solicit input from other team members to improve individual, as well as team, performance
- Initiate actions to resolve conflict
- Assert one's position/perspective in discussions about patient care (13)

Be the Change!

Though these principles from QSEN are relevant and must be incorporated into practice, before we choose to act intentionally against incivility in others, purposeful SELF-REFLECTION is needed (7). Because we can fail to see our own "blind spots," we must examine ourselves to see if we demonstrate any subtle form of bullying behaviors in our personal relationships or in the workplace. Have you been conditioned in any way to see bullying as acceptable and the norm? Recognize the deception that is often present in your own heart, and make needed changes personally before attempting to change others.

The article "Teaching Cognitive Rehearsal as a Shield for Lateral Violence: An Intervention for Newly Licensed Nurses" is a must read for any new nurse. It practically defines what professionalism in nursing practice looks like as well as a prepared plan to respond respectfully when bullying is directed toward you. Because bullying thrives in an environment of passivity where it has become normalized, it often stops when it is CONFRONTED in an assertive, direct, and respectful way (12). In one study where nurses were empowered by this strategy, 100 percent of the nurses reported that when the perpetrator was confronted, the bullying behavior stopped (10). This is the intervention that must be implemented if you experience bullying personally. For example, if a bullying nurse has a pattern of raising eyebrows or other nonverbal innuendo toward you, be prepared to respond in the following manner, "I sense (I see from your facial expression) that there may be something you wanted to say to me. Please speak directly to me" (12).

Embrace your ability to make a difference in your work environment! Influence your environment by modeling respect, embracing diversity, and forming meaningful relationships with your colleagues (12). Model and demonstrate professionalism in practice by never criticizing another colleague publicly, stand up for the absent colleague when they are not present, work as a team and accept your share of the workload (12).

If you continue to experience bullying or see it used against others and have confronted the perpetrator with no change in behavior, thoroughly document your concerns. Once adequate documentation has been collected, communicate your concerns to your nurse manager or human resources. In many cases nurse management is part of the problem by allowing bullying to continue unchallenged or they may be the perpetrator of bullying behaviors. In these circumstances human resources should be involved. Most institutions have policies regarding a healthy work environment free of hostility or violence of any kind that nurses can and should be held accountable to maintaining.

I have observed from my own experience that patient care units are like families, some are healthy and functional, while others are clearly dysfunctional and in need of intervention. Bullying is a toxic behavior that tends to be contagious and impacts everyone on that unit. Being a new nurse is like being in middle school again. You will want to do whatever it takes to fit in and be a part of the new group, even if it means being passive or indifferent to bullying behaviors around you. By being passive and doing nothing, you are actually part of the problem. Instead, hold yourself to the highest standards of professionalism in practice and be the change that is so desperately needed in nursing today!

Incivility in Nursing Education

Though these examples of incivility in the clinical setting are unsettling, our programs to educate nurses may also be part of the perpetuation and normalization of incivility that continues to persist today. The primary contributing factors are stress, disrespect, faculty arrogance, CONTROL, POWER, and a sense of student entitlement. When a culture of incivility is present, it causes emotional distress in students and is an active barrier to learning (14). Incivility can be defined as a disregard for others that creates a culture of disrespect, conflict, and stress (14). It simply boils down to which culture is dominant in your department; RESPECT vs. DISRESPECT. When mutual respect is not evident in faculty/student interactions, the bitter fruit of this seed will be incivility that begins with intense feelings of unfairness, anger, hostility, and even violence expressed toward faculty (14).

Incivility in academia has been likened to a "dance," one leads and the other follows. It is important that we do not point fingers and say this is a student or a faculty problem. In reality, uncivil behavior does not exist in a vacuum, but both students and faculty are partners and interdependent in this "dance" (14). When both students and faculty engage, communicate, and seek resolution of conflict before it digresses to incivility, a culture of respect and the "dance" of civility is present. But if opportunities to promote engagement by both faculty and students are missed, the root of disrespect is established and a "dance" of incivility is perpetuated. Once this dance has begun, regardless of who may be responsible for initiating it, incivility can escalate and become a blame game with no end in sight (14). Cynthia Clark has written and researched incivility at length in nursing education and has an excellent article series "Creating Communities of Civility." Let's look at the different relational contexts of incivility in nursing education: student to faculty, faculty to student, and faculty to faculty.

Bullying Behaviors: Student to Faculty

Entitlement and incivility have become increasingly pervasive in American society and contribute to incivility in nursing education (15). Unfortunately, students are not immune to this influence and reflect these attitudes as they enter nursing education. As a student or graduate nurse, did you bring attitudes that are also part of this problem? Did you come to your program with a sense of entitlement; that if you paid for an education, the college "owes" you a degree? Entitlement is expecting high grades for modest amounts of work, assuming a "consumer" mentality toward education, refusal to accept responsibility and making excuses for your failures. As a student, examine yourself to see if you are/were "uncivil" based on this list of the most common student incivility behaviors that nursing faculty identified (15).

- Disruptive behaviors in class/clinical that include:
    - Rude comments, engaging in side conversations, dominating class
    - Cell phone, texting, inappropriate computer use in class
    - Late to class and leaving early
    - Sleeping in class
- Anger or excuses for poor performance
- Inadequate preparation (14)
- Pressuring faculty until you get what you want (14)
- Bad mouthing other students, faculty, and the nursing program (14)

Contributing Factors

What is it that causes caring, empathetic nursing students to turn into uncivil beasts? Could the very culture of nursing education that prides itself on being highly competitive and academically rigorous be a contributing factor to student incivility? In one qualitative study the themes that students identified that contributed to incivility included burnout from demanding workloads and competition in a high-stakes academic environment (14). It appears the answer to the question is obvious, and it is imperative that nursing education as a whole examine the current paradigm and determine how students can be supported and nurtured within nursing education. Cynthia Clark has done extensive research on the topic of incivility in nursing education and has an excellent article for nursing students titled: "Cindy's "Five RITES" for fostering STUDENT-driven civility." In addition, there is an assessment tool, The Clark Academic Civility Index for Students, in this same article to determine if you are already or at risk of being an uncivil nurse once in practice (16).

Bullying Behaviors: Faculty to Student

Because it takes two to tango with the dance of incivility, we must take a closer look at the role of nursing faculty in this growing problem in academia. Research has confirmed that when incivility is experienced and directed toward students in nursing education, it "was often very hostile and soul destroying" (17). What is it that causes caring, empathetic nursing faculty to demonstrate incivility toward their students? In the same qualitative study, faculty identified STRESS as the primary problem. Ironically, nursing faculty are also burned out from their demanding workloads. Other causes of faculty stress include high faculty turnover, lack of qualified educators, role stress, and incivility from all sides: students, other faculty, and administration (14).

Both students and faculty identified several behaviors that communicate and demonstrate incivility as well. If you are an educator, examine and reflect to see if these behaviors of incivility are present in your classroom or clinical settings:

- Faculty superiority that is demonstrated by the following:
  - Exerting position and control over students (14)
  - Setting unrealistic student expectations (14)
  - Assuming a "know-it-all" attitude (14)
  - Being rigid, unapproachable, or rejecting students' opinions (18)
- Devaluing students' prior life experiences that can include work and academic experiences (14)
- Ineffective educators who cannot manage the classroom (14)
- Making condescending remarks or put-downs to students (18)
- Showing favoritism to certain students (14)
- Refusing or reluctant to answer questions (18)

There are two common denominators that both students and faculty have regarding the contributing factors to incivility: STRESS and DISRESPECT. Students are stressed by the juggling of many roles as provider/parent and student, as well as financial pressures and too little time. Faculty are stressed by multiple work demands, heavy workload, problematic students, and lack of faculty and needed support (15). The lack of respect by both faculty and students creates a poisonous, downward spiraling circle. If faculty are rigid, set unrealistic expectations, and do not allow open dialogue, students will inevitably respond with anger and lack of respect toward faculty, and a cycle of incivility is in motion. But it doesn't have to be this way; respect begets respect. If both faculty and students respectfully and openly communicate and engage with one another, a culture of civility can be nurtured instead (14).

How to Peacefully Coexist

Nursing academia ought to reflect the core values of the profession, which include caring, compassion, and nurturing of the other. Whether you are a nursing student or faculty, you can do your part to change the culture of your academic environment to make it a place where support and nurturing in a high stress/stakes environment is possible. To create a healthy culture, there must be a healthy relationship between both faculty and students. Therefore, the principles that apply to healthy personal relationships are relevant and also apply in academia. This includes the foundation of open/honest communication, working together, and establishing boundaries that are clearly defined and then enforced. If faculty implemented the following steps, civility can become normative:

1. Model caring and respect in all that you do so your students can see what true professionalism looks like in practice (15)!
2. Provide opportunities to dialogue with students in open formats, such as a town hall meeting format. This can provide needed dialogue and understanding (15).
3. Establish clearly written policies or place expectations in student code of conduct that address incivility, consequences, and then consistently enforce them (15).
4. Listen carefully; give students positive feedback (15).
5. Incorporate time management/stress reduction/self-care in the curriculum (15).
6. If constructive feedback is required for a student, the following approach will be helpful. Sandwich the comments: slice of bread (what student is doing well), middle peanut butter (something for the student to improve upon), and last slice of bread (what student is doing well). You will support and encourage your student when positive feedback and not just "needs to improve" comments are provided.

As a student, it is essential that you do your part, which includes:
1. Hold yourself to the highest standards of professionalism as a student, which includes:
    a. Be prepared, respectful, and engaged in your learning (18).
    b. Do not speak in a negative, derogatory manner openly about other STUDENTS, FACULTY, or the nursing PROGRAM.
    c. Abide consistently by the standards of student conduct of your institution.
2. Communicate your needs, and what you need/expect from faculty (18).
3. Work toward a common goal of civility and respect (18).

Principles of Respectful and Effective Communication

To complete this discussion on incivility, it is important to recognize that so much hinges on our words and how we communicate with one another. We must strive to be QUICK to listen and SLOW to speak! I have found the following principles of communication life-giving and restorative if they are used consistently in all that we say and do to our students and to one another. Solomon, the wisest man of ancient history, wrote the following words of wisdom in Proverbs that if put into practice will also work to recapture civility in nursing and nursing education:

- *Our words have power*
    - Life and death are in the power of the tongue. Use your words to bring healing, NOT to crush and to destroy the spirit of others (Proverbs 12:18).
    - *"Kind words heal and help; cutting words wound and maim"* (Proverbs 15:4).

- *The source of our words is important*
    - Be sure that what we speak does not provoke strife, but is based in truth, and that it is spoken in love.
    - *"It's a mark of good character to avert quarrels, but fools love to pick fights"* (Proverbs 20:3).

- *We must learn to listen*
    - Listen carefully to what is communicated. That is the only way you will learn and grow from constructive feedback.
    - *"The ear that listens to life-giving reproof will dwell among the wise"* (Proverbs 15:31).

- *THINK before you speak*
    - Becoming slow to anger is the beginning of wisdom (Proverbs 16:32).
    - *"The start of a quarrel is like a leak in a dam, so stop it before it bursts* (Proverbs 17:14).

- *Speak less*
    - Too much talking tends to digress in time to gossip. Let our words be few, and only what is needed.
    - *"But whoever restrains his lips is prudent"* (Proverbs 10:19).

- *Our tone matters*
    - *"A soft answer turns away wrath, but a harsh word stirs up anger"* (Proverbs 15:1).

Additional Resources to Promote Needed Change:

- Web Article: "Ten Ways to Reduce Incivility in Your Work Environment" by Rose O. Sherman

- Book: *Ending Nurse-to-Nurse Hostility: Why Nurses Eat Their Young and Each Other* by Kathleen Bartholomew

- Book: *When Nurses Hurt Nurses: Overcoming the Cycle of Nurse Bullying* by Cheryl Dellaseega

- Web Article: "What students can do to promote civility" by Cynthia Clark

For Faculty Only…

Bullying Behaviors: Faculty to Faculty

Though this book is focused on preparing students for professional practice, it is important to address one more aspect of incivility that has relevance to nursing education. This is the incivility that is present in the majority of nursing education departments (18). In one study only 5 percent felt that faculty worked well together (19). In a recent national study 68 percent of nursing faculty reported moderate to severe levels of faculty to faculty incivility. But when mild levels of faculty to faculty incivility are included, the prevalence of incivility in nursing academia rises to **96** percent (19)! Leading nurse educator and scholar Patricia Benner has made it clear that nursing education is in need of a RADICAL TRANSFORMATION, but in order to see this vision realized, it must first begin by seeing our nursing departments transformed through eliminating all vestiges of incivility!

Incivility in academia has been shown to lower job satisfaction, decrease productivity, and increase turnover (20). By allowing incivility to perpetuate as it has in the past, the anticipated nursing shortage will be exacerbated because of the inability to retain educators who, like myself, have a viable plan B called clinical practice if academia remains a hostile work environment. Because of the current nursing faculty shortage, in 2011, over 75,000 qualified nursing students were turned away in part because of lack of qualified faculty. Two-thirds of nursing programs surveyed indicated this was the primary contributing factor to not admitting all qualified students (22). There is a "perfect storm" brewing as the average age of associate professors is 57 (22) and the mean age of practicing registered nurses is 46 (21).

I have been amazed at the awareness and insightfulness that nursing students have regarding the presence of incivility among faculty. Though it may be thought to be successfully "hidden" from students' awareness, it typically is not. It is "caught" and an object of discussion among students. What is the "hidden" curriculum in our programs and what are we really teaching our students? Are educators guilty of normalizing incivility and accepting it as a fact of life of working in academia? Even if you are not experiencing incivility personally, if you are passive and tolerant when it is expressed toward other colleagues, you too are part of the problem.

Is your department part of the problem or part of the solution? Is your nursing department civil or uncivil? INCIVILITY according to Clark is defined as rude or disruptive behaviors that often result in psychological or physiological distress for the people involved and, if left unaddressed, may progress into threatening situations" (3). CIVILITY can be defined by "an authentic RESPECT for others during encounters of disagreement or controversy. It involves time, presence, and a willingness to engage in genuine discourse with the intention to seek common ground" (23). Examine yourself to see if any of these most commonly experienced examples of incivility in nursing education are present in you or others in your department:

- Persistent gossip, criticism, and insulting, demeaning remarks (15).
- Nonverbal disapproval in staff meetings that include eye rolling, arm crossing, walking out of meetings, and the use of the "silent treatment" (4).
- Avoidant, isolative, and exclusionary behaviors that marginalize (15).
- Setting others up to fail and intentional sabotage (15).
- Exerting superiority and rank over others/abuse of power (15).
- Not performing one's share of the workload (15).
- Department chair or senior faculty who use positional power to bully colleagues who are vulnerable due to their lower status in the department (20).

Transforming Academia

In one report, the key to cultivating civility in academia came down to three T's, truth telling, transparency, and tending to relationships (17).

1. **T**ruth Telling
    a. Be direct and honest in all communication with both faculty and students.
2. **T**ransparency
    a. Be willing to place in writing the standards as a faculty group that you want to establish regarding how to support one another during the school year or scholarly pursuits.
3. **T**ending to relationships
    a. A principle to live life by that can prevent the root of incivility from sprouting in your department is to not let the sun go down if you are still angry with a colleague. Deal with it that same day! Make the relationships in your department a priority, and nurture them so that the joy and passion that led you to become a nurse educator does not become derailed by incivility and hostile relationships.

My Story

As a nurse in the clinical setting for thirty years, I have experienced episodic incivility and bullying behaviors. When I entered nursing academia several years ago, I was totally unprepared for the intensity and severity of incivility that was unlike anything I had experienced in the clinical setting. These behaviors ranged from polarizing faculty attitudes toward the department chair, denigrating one another openly in faculty staff meetings, and withholding information that later led to intentional sabotage. My journey in nursing education at times has truly been a "broken road." It has been so painful that I have vowed not once, but twice to say "Never again" to continue my career as a nurse educator. I can make more money and have less stress and less pain in clinical practice! Although not all nursing academia institutions are like my experience; I can empathize with other faculty who have experienced this painful reality. But by the grace of God I am still standing and this book is a testimony to this reality. But there is more to my story. It is how God used one person to bring healing to a wounded soul.

Though I always enjoy presenting my topic of clinical reasoning at conferences, I had a cloud over me when I came to Elsevier's Faculty Development Institute last year (2013). I was deeply wounded by the incivility I had recently experienced in academia. Patricia Benner was the keynote speaker and I brought my well-marked copy of *Educating Nurses* to be signed by her, which she graciously did the day before! I had a well-received breakout session on "Clinical Reasoning in the Clinical" that situated clinical reasoning and the recommendations from Patricia Benner and her coauthors from *Educating Nurses*. I finished my session and several educators made their way up front to talk with me.

Another educator approached from a distance and also made her way up front. Other educators who saw her coming moved out of the way to let her come to meet me. All she said was, "We need to talk, and I would like to know if we could meet for lunch." Since it was time for the lunch break, I quickly said yes because I recognized her from our prior meeting. It was Patricia Benner! She had been in the audience for my session unknown to me and wanted to let me know what she thought of my presentation on her work (she liked it!). But this is not about having lunch with a living legend, but how God used her in my life to bring healing to my heart. Though other educators I had worked with did not value me and my contributions, Patricia Benner validated and affirmed me and let me know what she thought of my true worth and value as an educator during our time together.

Words That Bring Healing

I share this to highlight something that I think is important for each of us as faculty to recognize: the power of validation and encouragement to one another. In my experiences in academia, praise and affirmation were in short supply and rarely offered. We don't seem to recognize the power that this has to bring healing to hearts that have been wounded by incivility or are needed in a high stakes and stressful work environment.

Practical steps to transform the culture of a department where incivility is present takes time, patience, courage, and commitment to change by the entire department. The first and most effective, but also the most difficult, step is to respectfully CONFRONT in private an uncivil colleague. It can effectively put an end to the problem by directly addressing the behavior (4). Strong visionary leadership by the department chair or dean is also essential to lasting change.

The "elephant in the room" must be identified and called by its true name. If the "elephant in the room" is the department chair, then there may be more documentation needed to support your claim with administration. Each faculty member must make a renewed commitment to become more engaged and treat one another with dignity and respect (18). More importantly, if we have been a sword that has wounded others through our sharp words, we must be willing to humble ourselves and offer forgiveness to those we have wounded. Though this is difficult, this is how the power of a culture of incivility can be broken!

If incivility continues to flourish behind the doors of academia, many qualified and clinically current educators will likely leave as a result. Recognizing what is at stake, literally the ability to attract and retain qualified faculty to train the next generation of professional nurses because of the ongoing faculty shortage, it is my hope and prayer that grace and forgiveness would flow freely in our departments to bring needed healing to those we work with, those we teach, as well as our profession.

Additional Resources to Promote Needed Change:

Cynthia Clark, whose research is cited extensively in this section has several excellent web-based articles that can be accessed directly through these links and are an excellent supplement to further your knowledge and understanding on incivility, but more importantly, be a part of the needed change!

- Web Article: "The sweet spot of civility: My story" by Cynthia Clark
- Web Article: "Why civility matters by Cynthia Clark Article: What educators can do to promote civility" by Cynthia Clark
- Web Article: "From incivility to civility: Transforming the culture" by Cynthia Clark
- Web Article: "Conceptual model to promote civility in nursing education" by Cynthia Clark
- Book: *Creating & sustaining civility in nursing education* by Cynthia Clark
- Website: Civility Matters: Creating and sustaining communities of civility http://hs.boisestate.edu/civilitymatters/

Appendix B

Skeletons in the Closet: Men in Nursing

The male experience in nursing and nursing education has been very different from that of women in the modern era since the reforms initiated by Nightingale. Don't believe me? Then let me ask a series of questions that will put this in perspective. If you are a woman who chose to become a nurse:

- Was it suggested you may be a lesbian or was your femininity questioned because you chose to enter the nursing profession?
- Were you cautious in how you touched male patients while caring for them because it could be interpreted as sexual?
- Did you feel uncomfortable and vulnerable while caring for women on a post-partum unit?
- Did you experience isolation and loneliness because in clinical and in practice there were so few women in the program?
- Did you feel especially visible as a student because you "stood out" and felt that the faculty singled you out in class or clinical?

As a woman this was likely NOT your experience. Yet, if you are a man who chose to enter nursing, you can readily identify and have likely experienced many of these barriers as a student and then in practice (1). Was it coincidental that the comedy "Meet the Parents" was hugely successful in part because it played off the gender stereotypes of men in nursing by the lead character GAYlord Focker? Would it surprise you to realize that the earliest recorded caregivers were men and that men have a rich legacy of caregiving throughout world history? Let's take a brief walk through history, starting with the BCE era, that will take us from the past to the present to put today's male participation in perspective. If you would like to dig deeper on this rich topic, a much more thorough summary of the history of men in nursing can be found in the book *Men in Nursing: History, Challenges, and Opportunities*.

History

The earliest nurses in recorded history were male caregivers. In Hippocratic writings in ancient Greece, public nursing care was provided by men (2). In India around 275 BC, public hospitals were developed where men were the primary caregivers. In ancient Rome, the best possible care was provided to soldiers in military hospitals. Male nurses called "nosocomi" were the primary caregivers. This is also the root word for hospital or "nosocomial" acquired infection (3). The early Christian church had male deacons as well as female deaconesses who were responsible for ministering and caring for those who were ill (4).

In early Christian Greece and Rome, orders of monks known as Parabolani provided care for the ill (4). Historical accounts of the monastic movement show that men were responsible for the nursing care of the sick, wounded and dying as early as the fourth century. Military orders of knights were founded in the eleventh century, and some orders defended Jerusalem during the Crusades. The order of the Camellians founded by St. Camillus de Lellis, who served in the fifteenth century, had a symbol for his order, the red cross, that remains the primary symbol of healthcare today (5). Men also participated in nonmilitary orders during this time up until the sixteenth century when monastery orders were dissolved (6).

Nightingale: Not a "Fan"

"Though no one individual was more responsible for ushering in a period of female domination of nursing than Nightingale" (3, p.323), there were other social and cultural forces in the mid-1800s that also contributed to the lack of men who chose to enter the nursing profession. These social forces included the decline of male monastery orders that began in the 1500's with the Protestant Reformation, the increase in the number of convents and female nursing orders, and the Industrial Revolution of the 1800's that attracted men for its higher pay and no demand for formal education (3).

When Nightingale instituted the modern era of nursing, she chose to firmly establish it as a woman's occupation. To her, "every woman was a nurse," and a woman who entered nurse training was doing only what came naturally (6). European religious sisterhoods also embraced Nightingale's reforms, which by their very nature were exclusive to women (4).

Nightingale believed that men have no place in nursing "except where physical strength was needed" (7) and that men's "hard and horny" hands were not fit to touch, bathe, and dress wounded limbs however gentle their hearts may be (2). In England during the late 1800s, men who remained in nursing were excluded from general nursing practice as well as Nightingale's schools of nursing. The only practice environment available to men was in the insane asylums where men were needed because of their superior strength to restrain violent patients. The psychiatric education of men was considered inferior in length and quality in comparison to the women who attended Nightingale's schools of nursing (6). If a man wanted to expand his learning to include obstetrics and maternal-child nursing he was perceived as a pervert and threatened with expulsion (4).

Institutional/Educational Bias

By 1900 in England, general hospitals were dominated by female nurses. By 1919, the General Nursing Council (the equivalent of our current state boards of nursing), offered full membership only to women who were "general trained." Since most men were not able to even be admitted to these schools, nursing consolidated their position as the first self-determining female profession (8). Men comprised only 0.004 percent of nurses in England from 1921–1938 until the laws were changed to allow schools to accept men in 1947 (8).

In the United States, male nurses were excluded from membership in professional organizations such as the American Nurses Association that was founded in 1897. African-American nurses faced no similar bias. Men continued to be barred from the ANA until 1930 when the official position of the ANA was changed to strongly support men in nursing (3). National laws that were in place between 1901–1955 prevented men from serving as nurses in the United States Army Nurse Corps. It was only after the Korean War that this policy was changed. This continued to lower male participation in nursing in the United States so that by 1930, less than 1 percent of nurses were men (4).

Social/Cultural Barriers to Men in Nursing

Though the discriminatory policies of the past were a contributing factor to the small number of men in nursing, why don't more men seriously consider entering the nursing profession today? Numerous studies have addressed this topic and the barriers that men most commonly identified include (9):

- Traditional feminine image of nursing
- Lack of status
- Homosexual stereotype of male nurses
- Lack of awareness of wide range of opportunities
- The name of the profession…NURSE!

I find it fascinating that words do have power and carry strong associations. In one study of 100 male high school students, the number of male students who would consider nursing increased from six to twenty-one when nursing was renamed by the gender neutral title "registered clinician" (3). Does nursing leadership have the will and desire to even consider renaming the profession to remove this barrier? When women have recently entered heavily dominated male professions such as police and fire, the traditional policeMAN and fireMAN have been replaced with the gender neutral titles of police officer and firefighter.

Additional themes that are barriers to men considering nursing include gender role strain/or conflict, sexual identity, vulnerability and concerns over the sexualization of intimate touch, and gender stereotypes. These barriers have the consequence of distorting the view of nursing and result in most men not even considering nursing as a career choice (10). It has been reported that if men entered nursing at the same rate as women, there would be no nursing shortage (13).

Benefits to Being a Male Nurse

It is important to clearly communicate that men also have some unique advantages and benefits that women do not have in the nursing profession. The literature identifies several and I will share some of my own observations to provide some needed balance on this hot topic!

One of the most obvious benefits that I have observed and personally experienced as a male nurse is the "instant credibility" men tend to have with physicians in comparison to female nurses, even if you have limited clinical experience. Women I have worked with have expressed their frustration over the need to "prove" themselves as a capable caregiver when communicating with physicians. In comparison, there is an ease that male nurses have with physicians in establishing credibility to readily consider their "recommendations" that appear to be based primarily on the gender of the nurse. One researcher identified that the quality of the nurse-physician relationship was superior with men in comparison to female nurses. Physicians also perceived male nurses as more competent (11).

Because of the minority status of men in nursing, there is also a benefit in being the "token" male. In other words, doors tend to open more quickly and easily for certain positions that men have historically been seen as a professional "fit." This includes leadership and management positions. The nonsupportive treatment and even hostility that many women have experienced entering male-dominated professions is not present for most men in nursing (12). In one study, the "hidden" advantages to men in nursing included:

- Hiring preference over women
    - Masculine stereotypes that work to men's advantage include leadership ability, technical prowess, and physical strength
- Move up the ladder more quickly in leadership/management positions
    - Because majority of non-nursing management are also men, men are considered and promoted in part because they can relate to another man more effectively (11)

Men+Nursing=Great Fit!

Though I literally stumbled into the nursing profession by chance, from my vantage point of working in a wide variety of clinical settings, I strongly encourage men to consider nursing because of the wide variety of clinical opportunities that are an excellent fit for how men are wired. Deep in the male psyche is the need to have a battle to fight and an adventure to live by (19). Though you will see men in nursing practice in almost every clinical area, you will find the highest concentration in these clinical areas: ED, critical care, and nurse anesthetists. What do these three clinical areas all have in common? There is a lack of association with feminine nursing traits, such as touch and the delivery of intimate nursing care (12). In other words, they are HIGH tech, LOW touch specialties. In these clinical areas men tend to create "islands of masculinity" within the profession (12).

Another theme of these clinical areas is that they have high degrees of technology, adversity, autonomy, and high levels of acuity where the nurse can make a difference and literally save a life. There is a battle to fight and an adventure lived in these clinical areas. These themes run deep in the heart of a man (19) and are personally affirming and rewarding when one overcomes the most extreme clinical challenges. This truth can also be seen in the story of the Good Samaritan discussed in chapter 1. The Samaritan was also a MAN who saw a need (battle to fight), gave himself to help another at great personal risk and financial expense to himself (adventure to live by).

Let's engage in some higher level critical thinking by comparing and contrasting ED and ICU, and let me share what I know about each of these clinical specialties to see if you want to consider pursuing the unique battles and adventures they represent regardless of your gender!

	Emergency Department	**Critical Care**
Adversity	HIGH! Constant turnover of patients with a wide variety of acuity and always the potential for a crisis, either because of the volume of patients or the "stab" patient just brought in by the ambulance.	INTERMEDIATE Though these patients are critical, many are clinically stable despite being on a ventilator, vaso-active gtts etc. You can never let down your guard because things can change quickly!
Autonomy	INTERMEDIATE Though the physician writes orders and directs care, the nurse is the FIRST to assess the patient and with a wide variety of standing orders available to the nurse, needed interventions can be promptly initiated by the nurse!	HIGH As the primary nurse you are the eyes and ears for the physician who typically rounds once daily. If something begins to change in the status of your patient, it is your responsibility to identify it! Physicians expect the nurse to demonstrate high levels of autonomous critical thinking.
Acuity	INTERMEDIATE Despite the ongoing crisis of life in the ED portrayed by shows such as *ER*, this is NOT reality. The majority of patients seen in ED are nonlife threatening and NOT critical.	HIGH Every patient is critical and has the potential to QUICKLY deteriorate. High level of vigilance is always required by the nurse.
Technology	MODERATE Adrenaline is always flowing but is not a high tech area unless there is a "stab" patient who is on a ventilator or a full arrest initiating "cool-it" protocol.	HIGH Technologies such as mechanical ventilators and intra-aortic balloon pumps, continuous cardiac output monitors and monitors that display CVP, PA, and art-line pressures are standard.

Strategies for a Successful Transition to Practice

If you are a male student or new nurse, below are some general principles that I have found beneficial as a male member of the profession to engage and transition to a work culture that is predominantly female:

- *Find common ground with the women you work with.*
    - Though you may not be able to identify with some of the intimate, personal things that women often share with one another and you will likely overhear, be intentional to find what you do have in common. You will be tempted at times to disengage and run feeling frustrated that no one seems to show an interest in sports, hunting, etc. But if you have children or pets, these topics are common ground that you can steer the conversation toward and build bridges whenever possible!

- *Be a team player.*
    - This is another way to intentionally engage with the women you work with. Make yourself consistently available by offering help of any kind whenever you have time. Though men sometimes get asked to literally do the "heavy lifting" on the unit, this assistance is always appreciated and again is a practical way to build a bridge.

- *Celebrate diversity!*
    - This cuts both ways for men and women. Much of the incivility in nursing is a result of not valuing and respecting the unique gender differences of men and women. The direct communication styles of men can create an offense to other women, even though it was respectful. Make it a priority to accept the gender distinctives of the opposite sex. Do not be critical of men because they are not more like women and vice versa!

I have addressed and documented the male experience in nursing at length because it is imperative that both men and women recognize that nursing is not a feminine profession. Men have played heroic roles as care providers over the last 2500 years. Though bias well documented in the past, it still lingers today. I want to encourage men to recover caregiving and nursing as a career option. Men as well as ethnic minorities are an untapped resource that will be needed in the future to meet the demands of the nursing as well as nursing faculty shortage.

Additional Resources:

- Book: *Men in Nursing: History, Challenges, and Opportunities by* Chad O'Lynn /Russell Tranbarger
- Book: *MAN UP! A practical guide for men in nursing* by Christopher Lance Coleman
- Website: American Assembly for Men in Nursing: http://aamn.org/

For Faculty Only…

Men & Nursing Education

Quantitative research has shown that the barriers men face in nursing education are "pervasive, consistent, and have changed little over time" (13). Though overt bias is rare, covert discrimination is much more common. One way this more subtle form of discrimination manifests itself is the feminine emphasis on how to provide care. The underlying message to male students is that in order to be a nurse, you have to behave like a woman (14). In addition, nursing textbooks have limited or excluded historical male contributions to nursing while emphasizing those of women. This revision of nursing history perpetuates the myth that nursing has always been a female dominated profession (15).

Nursing faculty may also be inadvertently part of the problem. Men perceive an inherent bias in education with feelings of isolation and loneliness exacerbated by the lack of male faculty who serve as role models, as well as the use of the pronoun "she" and assumption that nursing is a feminine profession. In addition, the pedagogies used in education emphasize feminine learning styles, communication strategies, personal reflection, and methods of caring (16).

Male students quickly realize that if they are assertive or question faculty (traditional masculine traits) they are stigmatized, and they recognize the need to temper their masculine behavior and act more feminine to "fit in." Not surprisingly, the attrition rate of men in nursing education in one study was almost three times the rate of women (10). Higher rates of attrition for men have been well documented in other studies as well. Though there is an assumption by some faculty that men who enter nursing are doing so primarily for financial gain, the motivation for men to enter nursing is similar to women: the desire to help others, a sense of calling, and job security (10, 17).

In one survey of male nursing students, these were the most commonly felt and experienced barriers by men in nursing education:

- No history of men in nursing presented in textbooks.
- Textbooks referred to the nurse as "she."
- Exclusive use of lecture format in classroom.
- No male faculty and no opportunity to work with male nurses in clinical setting (13).

How Nurse Educators Can "Be the Change"

If you are a nurse educator you can warm the climate for men in your program. Based on current research, the following simple steps can make this warming front a reality! The following best practices from the literature are a good place to begin this needed discussion. Reflect on the content of this appendix to help assess if your program is "cold" or "warm" towards men to promote their retention and success:

1. *Men and women have different brains and learn differently!*
   - Because of the difference in learning styles, changes to pedagogy and curricula should be considered if there is a strong emphasis on feminine styles of learning (20).
   - Women tend to be relational learners and prefer large amounts of reading assignments, while more men are independent learners and prefer APPLIED learning strategies. Therefore, lecture-only format was found to be a barrier to learning by men (21). Mix it up with active learning strategies such as clinical reasoning case studies in the classroom and this barrier can be removed!

2. *Men benefit from the support of other men.*
   - Therefore, clinical placements should be done with other male students as much as possible and to place male students with a male instructor or a male nurse on the floor if possible to promote needed role modeling and additional support (20).

3. *Provide instruction in the curricula regarding the use of touch and provision of intimate touch while providing care* (18).
   - Though this is needed for all students, it is especially relevant for men who report feeling "vulnerable" in this aspect of patient care.

4. *Provide instruction in the curricula to prepare men to work with women.*
   - This should also include the differences in communication styles between men and women.

5. *Provide instruction in fundamentals curricula regarding the history of nursing and the role of men in nursing as caregivers* (9).
   - Textbooks have neglected or de-emphasized this historical reality. Make it a priority to re-cover this needed emphasis to demonstrate that in the big picture of history, nursing truly is a gender-neutral profession. The role of Florence Nightingale that resulted in the marginalization of men as caregivers must also is relevant to both men and women in nursing education. The historical summary in this chapter can be a needed springboard to this needed discussion!

6. *Ensure the perception that nursing is a diverse, gender-neutral profession.*
    o   Examine your school's recruitment material to make sure it contains both men, women, and ethnic minorities. Collaborate with the guidance counselors at the high school in your community to see if they are providing accurate information to male students regarding nursing as an appropriate career choice for both men and women and that men are not discouraged from considering nursing (1).

7. *Meticulously examine nursing textbooks and curricula for a "hidden curriculum" that through the use of gender pronouns such as "she" communicate that nursing is for women only* (10).
    o   Once identified, eliminate them or use material that does not reinforce this stereotype.

8. *ALLOW MEN TO BE MEN.*
    o   Do not take assertive behavior personally. This is how men are wired and as long as all communication is done respectfully, do not discourage or communicate that this is not acceptable.

Appendix C

Practical Preparation to Pass the NCLEX

Perhaps some of you have yet to take your state licensure boards, the final step for you to enter into professional practice. Did you know that starting April 1, 2013, an already difficult test just got harder? Due to the continuous changes in US healthcare and nursing practice, the National Council of State Boards of Nursing (NCSBN) has determined that entry-level RN practice requires a greater level of knowledge, skills, and abilities than was previously required, resulting in the passing standard increase. The passing standard will change from the current -0.16 logits (a logit is defined as a unit of measurement to report relative differences between candidate ability estimates and item difficulties) to 0.00 logits. It is expected to DECREASE current pass rates as well (1).

Categories of NCLEX and Percentages of Content

The NCLEX has a predictable blueprint (NCLEX-RN Test Plan) that consists of four major categories of client needs. It also has a predictable percentage of content for each category. Two of these major categories are divided for a total of six subcategories for a total of eight categories of content. This is the current NCLEX blueprint that includes the percentage of content, a brief definition, and the most common concepts that will be situated in each category:

I. Safe and Effective Care Environment
   a. 20%–Management of Care
      i. Providing and directing nursing care that enhances the care delivery setting to protect clients, family/significant others, and healthcare personnel
         1. Establish priorities
         2. Collaboration w/treatment team
         3. Advocacy
   b. 12%–Safety and Infection Control
      i. Protecting clients, families, and healthcare personnel from health and environmental hazards
         1. Error prevention
         2. Safe use of equipment
         3. Injury prevention

II. Health Promotion & Maintenance:
      i. 9%–The nurse provides and directs nursing care of the client and family/significant others that incorporates knowledge of expected growth and

development principles, prevention and/or early detection of health problems, and strategies to achieve optimal health.
1. Disease prevention
2. Physical assessment
3. Client education

III. Psychosocial Integrity:
   i. 9%–Nurse provides care that promotes and supports the emotional, mental, and social well-being of the patient and family who are experiencing stressful events.
      1. Coping mechanisms
      2. Therapeutic communication
      3. End of life care

IV. Physiologic Integrity
   a. 9%–Basic Care & Comfort:
      i. Providing comfort and assistance in the performance of activities of daily living
         1. Elimination
         2. Nutrition/oral hydration
         3. Mobility/immobility
   b. 15%–Pharmacological & Parenteral Therapies:
      i. Providing care related to the administration of medications and parenteral therapies
         1. Expected actions, adverse/side effects
         2. Medication administration
         3. IV therapies
         4. Dosage calculation
   c. 12%–Reduction of Risk Potential:
      i. Reducing the likelihood that clients will develop complications or health problems related to existing conditions, treatments or procedures
         1. Changes in VS
         2. Diagnostic tests
         3. Lab values
         4. System specific assessments
         5. Potential for alterations in body systems
   d. 13%–Physiological Adaptation:
      i. Managing and providing care for clients with acute, chronic, or life threatening health conditions.
         1. Pathophysiology
         2. F&E imbalances
         3. Medical emergencies (2)

As you reflect upon your personal current strengths and weaknesses of content knowledge based on this NCLEX blueprint, it is my recommendation that you make it your top priority to focus on your weaknesses and make them a strength! For further information on the NCLEX, see the official website of the National Council of State Boards of Nursing at: https://www.ncsbn.org.

Though this book is intended to prepare you for professional practice, it will also help prepare you to pass the NCLEX examination (I still recommend an NCLEX review text or review course!). How is this possible? Because every question on the NCLEX is situated around a brief clinical scenario and the correct response is derived from this clinical context. Each clinical reasoning case study in this book is drawn from a clinical practice context as well. Every clinical reasoning question in the case studies, as well as the NCLEX, will require APPLICATION to the context of a clinical scenario. The NCLEX will require you to demonstrate your ability to identify RELEVANT assessment data and identify the nursing PRIORITY (no NANDA statements are used in the NCLEX), PRIORITY nursing interventions, and clinical data that reflects a complication (remember Jason!) that must be identified.

Application/Analysis Knowledge Required!

Lower levels of thinking are knowledge and comprehension. Though this is important, if this is the highest level of knowledge you possess on content from nursing education, you will FAIL the NCLEX. You MUST be able to APPLY knowledge and analyze data to identify the correct nursing priority or nursing intervention. To compare and contrast these two levels of knowledge I will use a couple test questions that I have developed. The first question is an example of the lower level of knowledge/comprehension:

1. What pharmacologic category does atenolol belong to?
    a. Calcium channel blocker
    b. ACE inhibitor
    c. Beta blocker
    d. Nitrates

If you chose (c.) beta blocker, you are correct! This was straightforward knowledge, and probably too easy for most.

Let's look at the higher level thinking required to pass the NCLEX. Application is the ability to APPLY your knowledge to a clinical context. Analysis includes the ability to compare and contrast information and deduce the correct response. This is high level thinking that requires DEEP UNDERSTANDING of the content so you can readily apply it to the wide variety of clinical situations you will see in practice. This is the bar that must be met in order to pass the NCLEX. Let's do a test question using this level of knowledge and see if you find it a bit more difficult.

2. In your patient with heart failure, which of the following medications is the BEST choice to lower blood pressure?
    a. Atenolol (Tenormin)
    b. Diltiazem (Cardizem)
    c. Labetolol (Trandate)
    d. Lisinopril (Prinivil)

In order to come to the correct response you must UNDERSTAND the mechanism of action of each of these medications and more importantly UNDERSTAND the pathophysiology to choose the correct answer. Knowing that this patient has heart failure, we must contextualize our knowledge to this condition. Based on your knowledge of the pathophysiology of heart failure, medications that have a negative inotropic effect on the heart may exacerbate heart failure and should be used with caution. You know that atenolol (Tenormin) and labetolol (Trandate) are both beta blockers; they block beta stimulation to the heart. Does this result in a negative inotropic effect or decreased contractility? Absolutely! So we can eliminate these two medications.

Does diltiazem (Cardizem) affect cardiac contractility? You know that it is a calcium channel blocker, but does this category of cardiac drugs decrease contractility? Knowing the role of calcium in cardiac pathophysiology, YES, the blockage of calcium does produce a negative inotropic effect and should be eliminated. This leaves Lisinopril (Prinivil), an ACE inhibitor. Knowing that an ACE inhibitor blocks the conversion of angiotensin I to angiotensin II and causes as a result arterial vasodilation that lowers afterload and decreases cardiac workload with no negative inotropic effect on the heart, this is clearly the BEST and correct answer. Did you find this a more difficult question? If so, you have much to learn to prepare for the NCLEX as well as clinical practice!

Remember that every NCLEX question is situated with a clinical scenario. For each question you will be expected to use application and analysis level of thinking to know one or more of the following to choose the correct answer:
1. *What is the best clinical judgment to make?*
2. *What is the nursing priority?*
3. *What is the rationale for every nursing intervention or physician order?*
4. *What is the expected outcome for any medication or physician order?*
5. *Within the context of the clinical scenario, what clinical data is significant and relevant?*
6. *What are the most common laboratory values and the nursing implications if they are abnormal?*

- You must also memorize the normal ranges of these common laboratory values because the NCLEX question will only give you a value, you must interpret it!
7. *Compare/contrast normal physical assessment findings with those that are abnormal, and then reflect and see if these abnormal findings are clinically significant.*
8. *Compare/contrast normal vital sign findings with those that are abnormal, and then reflect and see if these abnormal findings are clinically significant.*
    - You must also know the VS normal ranges not only for adults, but also infants and children because when clinical data is presented, you need to interpret it based on your knowledge of these norms.

Are you overwhelmed yet? This is a high order of mastery for any new graduate! You may not feel you were adequately prepared for this level of knowledge and clinical practice. The clinical reasoning case studies I have constructed reflect real-world practice and incorporate these key NCLEX objectives that correlate with an emphasis of clinical reasoning in practice. If you make it a priority to APPLY and translate the content of your nursing program to the bedside, and if you work through the case studies that I have created and then carefully review the answer key that contains well-developed rationale, you are well on your way to being prepared not only for the NCLEX, but more importantly the rigors of professional practice!

Additional Resources:
- Website: National Council of State Boards of Nursing: https://www.ncsbn.org/index.htm
- Web Article: "Talking Points to the 2013 NCLEX-RN Passing Standard"

Clinical Handouts to Prepare You for Practice

Over the last several years I have responded to the needs of my students who needed something simple to help them understand and master difficult but essential content. These handouts have been "field tested" and have been found beneficial by my students to promote learning. They are provided here to help you as well! You have my permission to copy any of the following worksheets to promote your learning as well!

- **Appendix D: Medications That Must Be Mastered Worksheet**
  - To strengthen your knowledge and understanding of medications, use this worksheet starting with any medications from the most common forty-five meds referenced in chapter 2 or any other medications that may be a weakness to make them your strength.

- **Appendix E: Laboratory Tests That Must Be Mastered Worksheet**
  - To strengthen your knowledge and understanding of lab values, use this worksheet with any labs that are currently a weakness to make them your strength! This worksheet was referenced in chapter 2–The Applied Sciences.

- **Appendix F: Patient Preparation Worksheet**
  - If you have yet to develop your own personal patient prep worksheet to use in practice, I have used a similar worksheet for years and found it to work well to schedule my day, capture trends and patient care priorities by comparing most recent VS and assessment findings as well as second page with clinical reasoning questions to help establish nursing priorities and plan of care. The second page is optional depending on your needs.

- **Appendix G: Clinical Lab Values and Nursing Responsibilities**
  - This handout simplifies NEED TO KNOW knowledge and helps build a plan of care around abnormal, relevant lab values.
  - Based on abnormal lab findings, what are the essential nursing assessments that need to be implemented so you can begin to do "lab planning"?

- **Appendix H: Most Commonly Used Categories of Medications**
  - With over 5,000 meds used in clinical practice, this handout simplifies needed medication knowledge by grouping the most commonly used meds by category, class, most common side effects, and relevant nursing implications.

- **Appendix I: Comprehending Cardiac Medications**:
  - Review of preload, afterload, and contractility and how different cardiac meds and their classes (ACE-I, B-blockers, diuretics, etc.) influence these determinants of cardiac output. This content must be understood to promote higher level critical thinking with your patients who receive the most common cardiac medications.

- **Appendix J: Clinical Reasoning Questions to Develop Nurse Thinking**
  - Identifies seven PRE-clinical questions and four-DURING clinical questions to promote nurse thinking as well as two questions to develop nurse caring and engagement. Same questions are used in the case studies but this template readily transfers to clinical practice.

Appendix D
Medications That Must Be Mastered Worksheet

Name	Dose: High-low-avg.?	Pharm. Class	Therapeutic use/ Mech. Of action	Adverse actions (most common SE)	Nursing Implications… What must be known before giving? or assessed afterwards?

Appendix E
Lab Planning: Laboratory Tests That Must Be Mastered Worksheet

Lab Value	Normal value Critical value	Why Relevant?	Nsg. Assessments/interventions required:

Lab Value	Normal value Critical value	Why Relevant?	Nsg. Assessments/interventions required:

Lab Value	Normal value Critical value	Why Relevant?	Nsg. Assessments/interventions required:

Lab Value	Normal value Critical value	Why Relevant?	Nsg. Assessments/interventions required:

Lab Value	Normal value Critical value	Why Relevant?	Nsg. Assessments/interventions required:

Appendix F: Patient Preparation Worksheet

Time	Meds/Care Priorities	Misc.

Adm. Date_____ POD#_____

Chief Complaint/Primary Problem:

Past Medical History

	CV	Resp	Neuro	GI	GU	Skin/Pain	Misc.	VS
Prior Nursing Assessment >>>								
Current Nursing Assessment >>>								

Lab Test	Current	Most Recent
Na+		
K+		
Mg+		
Creat.		
WBC		
Neut. %		
Hgb.		

Allergies_____
_____
Code Status_____
IV site_____
IV Maintenance_____
IV Drips_____
Activity_____
Fall Risk/Safety_____
Diet_____
Bladder/Bowel_____
_____
_____
_____

End of Shift SBAR

Situation:

Background:

Assessment:

Recommendation:

Appendix F: Patient Worksheet page 2:
Clinical Reasoning Questions to Develop Nurse Thinking
(Formulate and reflect before and after report, but BEFORE seeing patient the first time)

1. What is the primary problem and what is the underlying cause/pathophysiology of this problem?

2. What clinical data from the chart is RELEVANT and needs to be trended because it is clinically significant?

3. What nursing priority will guide your plan of care?

4. What nursing interventions will you initiate based on this priority and what are the desired outcomes?

5. What body system(s) will you focus on based on your patient's primary problem or nursing care priority?

6. What is the worst possible/most likely complication(s) to anticipate based on the primary problem?

7. What nursing assessments will you need to initiate to identify this complication if it develops?

While Providing Care...*(Review and note during shift after initial patient assessment)*
8. What clinical assessment data did you just collect that is RELEVANT and needs to be TRENDED because it is clinically significant to detect a change in status?

9. Does your nursing priority or plan of care need to be modified in any way after assessing your patient?

10. After reviewing the primary care providers note, what is the rationale for any new orders or changes made?

11. What educational/discharge priorities have you identified and how will you address them?

Caring and the "Art" of Nursing
12. What is the patient likely experiencing/feeling right now in this situation?

13. What can I do to engage myself with this patient's experience, and show that he/she matters to me as a person?

Appendix G: Clinical Lab Values and Nursing Responsibilities

	Patho	Ranges	Causes	Treatments	Nsg. Considerations
I. Blood Chemistries **Sodium: Hyponatremia** Normal: 135-145 mEq/L	*Most abundant cation in EXTRAcellular fluid *Maintains osmotic pressure of extracellular fluid *Regulates renal retention & excretion of water *Responsible for stimulation of neuromuscular reactions & maintains SBP	Serum below 135mEq/L **Critical RED FLAG:** **<120**	*Excess sodium loss through N-V-D, skin and kidneys *Excess diuretic dosage *Liver Failure *CHF *Increased hypotonic IV fluids	*Sodium containing IV fluids *Lactated Ringers *NS 0.9% or 3%	**THINK VOLUME** *Monitor electrolytes *Monitor vital signs *Monitor neurological responses *Mental Status *Headaches *Monitor fluids/I&O for overload *Weights daily *Cardiac overload-CHF *Monitor musculoskeletal-cramps/weakness/tremor
Sodium: Hypernatremia Normal: 135-145 mEq/L		Serum above 145 mEq/L **Critical RED FLAG:** **>160**	*Dehydration-fluid loss through N-V-D (water loss in excess of salt loss) or excessive sweating *Diabetes-DKA *Fever	*Replace fluids *D5% *Diuretics- Excrete excess volume and excrete (sodium is then concentrated with fluid volume deficit)	**THINK VOLUME** *Monitor electrolytes *Monitor vital signs *Mental Status *Weight/I&O *Monitor for seizures
Potassium: Hypokalemia Normal: 3.5-5.2 mEq/L	*Most abundant INTRAcellular cation and is essential for transmission of electrical impulses in cardiac and skeletal muscle *Helps maintain acid-base balance and has inverse relationship to metabolic pH…decrease in pH of 0.1 (acidosis) increases K+ by 0.6 mEq/L *80-90% K+ filtered through the kidney	Serum below 3.5 mEq/L **Critical RED FLAG:** **<2.5**	*Inadequate intake of K+ *ETOH abuse *CHF/HTN *GI Loss-V&D *Renal Loss *Diuretics-Loop: Furosemide (Lasix) Bumetadine (Bumex)	*Oral or Parenteral Potassium *Diet high in potassium *Balanced electrolyte solutions *Pedialyte *Sports drinks	**THINK ELECTRICITY** *Monitor electrolytes *Monitor vital signs-low BP *Monitor cardiac responses *Irregular heart rate and rhythm for increased ectopy-PVC's/VTach

	Patho	Ranges	Causes	Treatments	Nsg Considerations		
Potassium: Hyperkalemia Normal: 3.5-5.0 mEq/L		Serum above 5.0 mEq/ **Critical RED FLAG: >6**	*Metabolic acidosis *Dehydration *Excess potassium intake *Potassium sparing diuretics *Tissue damage-Burns (K+ goes out of cell) *Renal Failure	*Insulin- Moves K+ into the cell *D50- Prevents hypoglycemia caused by the infusion of Insulin *IV Calcium Gluconate also given at the same time to counteract cardiac effects of potassium *Sodium Bicarbonate- treats the acidosis caused when K+ moves into the cell and pushes hydrogen ions into the serum	**THINK ELECTRICITY** *Monitor electrolytes *Monitor cardiac responses *Monitor musculoskeletal cramps, weakness, parathesias *Peaked T wave/wide QRS *Monitor neurological responses, mental status, headache *Irregular heart rate and rhythm for increased ectopy-PVC's/Vtach		
Magnesium: Hypomagnesemia Normal: 1.6-2.6 mg/dL	*Second most abundant intracellular cation *Required for transmission of nerve impulses and muscle relaxation *Controls absorption of sodium, potassium, calcium, and phosphorus *Magnesium.Potassium and Calcium all go low or high together!	Serum below 1.6 mg/dL **Critical RED FLAG: <1.2**	*Chronic Alcoholism *GI Loss-V&D *Impaired absorption *Renal Disease *Pancreatitis	*Treat underlying cause *GI Loss *Give Magnesium replacement	**THINK NEUROMUSCULAR TRANSMISSION** **THINK CARDIAC RESPONSE** *Monitor electrolytes *Monitor vital signs *Tachycardia *Hypertension *Tremors, tetany, paresthesias *Muscle weakness		
Magnesium: Hypermagnesemia Normal: 1.6-2.6 mg/dL		Serum above 2.6 mg/dL **Critical RED FLAG: >6.1**	*Dehydration *Severe metabolic acidosis *Renal Failure *Tissue trauma	*Treat underlying cause *Renal patients treat with dialysis *Monitor cardiac effects of magnesium-increased PVC's-VT *Give Calcium Gluconate	**THINK NEUROMUSCULAR TRANSMISSION** **THINK CARDIAC RESPONSE** *Monitor electrolytes *Monitor vital signs *Bradycardia *Hypotension *Muscle weakness		

	Patho	Ranges	Causes	Treatments	Nsg Considerations
Calcium: Hypocalcemia Normal: 8.2-10.6 mg/dL	*Most abundant cation in body and necessary for almost all vital processes *Half of total body calcium circulates as free ions that participate in coagulation, neuromuscular conduction, intracellular regulation, control of skeletal and cardiac muscle contractility *98-99% calcium reserves stored in teeth and skeleton	Serum below 8.2 mg/dL **Critical RED FLAG:** <7	*ETOH abuse *Pancreatitis *Chronic renal failure Inadequate intake *Decreased Vitamin D (Sunshine) *Lack of weight bearing *Loop Diuretics *Hypomagnesemia 1q`	Oral Calcium carbonate/gluconate Calcium chloride (more irritating to the vein) Watch for extravasate into subcutaneous tissue	**THINK MUSCLE RESPONSE** *Monitor electrolytes *Monitor vital signs *Cardiac Output decreased *Hypotension *Dysrhythmias *Monitor neuromuscular responses: seizures, tetany, paresthesias, muscle spasms
Calcium: Hypercalcemia Normal: 8.2-10.6 mg/dL		Serum above 10.6 mg/dL **Critical RED FLAG:** >12	*Prolonged immobilization *Dehydration *Cancer *Excess Antacid Intake	*Eliminate Calcium through kidneys through IV fluids *Loop diuretic to promote elimination of calcium	**THINK MUSCLE RESPONSE** *Monitor electrolytes *Monitor vital signs Hypertension *Monitor GI: N&V-anorexia *Dysrhythmias
Creatinine Normal: 0.5-1.2 mg/dl	*End product of creatine metabolism which is performed in skeletal muscle *Small amount of creatine is converted to creatinine which is then secreted by kidneys *Amount of creatinine generated proportional to mass of skeletal muscle	Serum above 1.2 mg/dl *Gold standard for kidney function because creatinine is produced in consistent quantity and rate of clearance reflects glomerular filtration	**Decreased in:** Decreased skeletal muscle Inadequate protein intake **Increased in:** CHF Dehydration Acute & chronic renal failure Shock	Correct underlying problem Fluid resuscitation to keep SBP>90 Dialysis	**THINK FLUID BALANCE** *Assess I&O closely *Fluid restriction *Assess for signs of fluid retention/edema

	Patho	Ranges	Causes	Treatments	Nsg Considerations
Blood Urea Nitrogen (BUN) Normal: 10-20 mg/dl	Urea represents end product of protein metabolism performed in the liver Urea diffuses freely in intra/extracellular fluid and then excreted by kidneys BUN reflects balance between production and excretion of urea Ratio to creatinine is 15-24:1 (if creatine 1.0 expected BUN should be 15-24) Is indirect measurement of renal function but does not reflect glomerular filtration	**Critical RED FLAG:** >100	**Decreased in:** Poor protein intake/malnutrition Liver disease Malabsorption syndromes **Increased in:** Acute renal failure CHF Hypovolemia-dehydration Pyelonephritis Hyperalimentation/TPN	*Fluid resuscitation-HIGH *Dialysis-HIGH *Improve nutritional intake/Failure to thrive- LOW	**THINK FLUID BALANCE** *Assess I&O closely *Fluid restriction *Assess for signs of fluid retention/edema *Assess for agitation, confusion, fatigue, *N&V- HIGH *Assess liver profile labs for correlating liver damage
II. Hematology **Hemoglobin-HGB** Normal: Adult- 13-17 g/dl	*Primary protein of erythrocytes that is composed of heme (iron) and globin (protein) *Carries O2 to cells and CO2 back to lungs *Parallels Hematocrit which is the % of RBC in proportion to total plasma volume *GOLD Standard for evaluating blood/RBC adequacy (anemia, blood loss)	**Critical RED FLAG:** <6 or >18 *Range of Anemias:* **Mild** Hgb 10-12 g/dl- asymptomatic **Moderate:** Hgb 6-10 g/dl weakness, fatigue, palpitations, SOB, decreased tol to activity- orthostatic hypotension **Severe:** Hgb < 6 g/dl Hypoxia: confusion, SOB, skin pallor- and MM and nailbeds, dizziness, weakness, tachycardia	**Clinical Uses:** Detect blood loss, anemia and response to treatment Detect any possible blood disorder **Decreased in:** Anemia Cancer Fluid retention/overload Hemorrhage **Increased in:** COPD CHF Dehydration Polycythemia	*Correct underlying problem *Blood transfusions if symptomatic	**THINK BLOOD LOSS/ANEMIA** *Identify early signs of blood loss: tachycardia, then hypotension *Transfuse as needed- assess closely in first 30" for transfusion reactions *Assess for signs of tissue hypoxia (see above)

	Patho	Ranges	Causes	Treatments	Nsg Considerations
White Blood Cell Count (WBC) Normal: 4,500-11,000 mm3	*WBC represent primary defense against invading infections *This is a total count of all 5 leukocytes: neutrophils, lymphocytes, eosinophils, basophils, and monocytes *Indicates overall degree of bodies response to pathology, but must be evaluated and correlated through differential count *Elevated WBC due to significant increase in one differential-usually the neutrophil *Physiologic stress or steroids will increase WBC	**Critical RED FLAG:** <2500 or >15,000	**Decreased in:** ETOH abuse Anemia Bone marrow depression Viral infections **Increased in:** Infection Anemia Inflammatory disorders Steroid use (acute or chronic)	*Identify infectious process *Confirm bone marrow depression in chemo/radiation therapy	**THINK INFECTION** *Low or elevated WBC can represent sepsis *Assess closely for hypotension with known infection (septic shock) *Assess closely for any change in temperature trend-hypothermia or febrile can both represent sepsis especially in elderly
Neutrophils Normal: 50-70% of differential	*Most predominant differential WBC- comprise 50-70% of all WBC's *First line of defense against bacterial infection through phagocytosis (think pacman) ***BANDS**- if present on differential-correlate with overwhelming sepsis. Immature neutrophils body is kicking into circulation before they are ready because of the severity of infection/sepsis	**Critical RED FLAG:** >80%	**Increased in:** Infection Acute hemorrhage Physical stress Tissue necrosis/injury **Decreased in:** Bone marrow depression (chemo/radiation therapy) Viral infection (due to increased lymphocytes)	*Identify infectious process *Confirm bone marrow depression in chemo/radiation therapy	**THINK INFECTION** *Low or elevated WBC can represent sepsis *Assess closely for hypotension with known infection (septic shock) *Assess closely for any change in temperature trend-hypothermia or febrile can both represent sepsis especially in elderly

	Patho	Ranges	Causes	Treatment	Nsg Considerations
III. Cardiac **Troponin** Normal: <0.05 ng/ml This may vary depending on each hospital lab	*Contractile protein found in cardiac muscle that will be released into systemic circulation with cardiac ischemia or acute MI *Levels will rise 2-6 hours after injury-peak 16-24 hours and then remain elevated for several days *If acute onset CP to r/o MI they will be done every 6 hours x3 to determine pattern of abnormal elevation	Critical RED FLAG: ANY ELEVATION If elevated this establishes diagnosis of acute MI *If positive MI, the degree of elevation provides general barometer of degree of heart muscle damage	Increased in: Acute MI Unstable angina Minor myocardial damage after CABG or PTCA/stent placement	*Standards of cardiac care include continuous telemetry, b-blockers to decrease cardiac workload, heparin or nitroglycerin gtts. *Definitive treatment of MI includes PTCA/stent or CABG	THINK CARDIAC-MI *Assess closely for recurrent or new onset of chest pain *Assess cardiac rhythm for any changes such as PVC's, VTach or atrial fibrillation *Assess HR and SBP carefully to promote decreased cardiac workload (maintain heart rate <80 and SBP <140 *Assess tolerance to activity closely
Brain Natriuretic Peptide (BNP) Normal: <100 ng/L	*Hormone that is stored in the ventricle of the heart *When left ventricle is distended and stretched due to CHF exacerbation BNP is released into circulation Inhibits the release of renin by kidneys which promotes water and sodium loss as well as increases glomerular filtration rate (Body's own ACE inhibitor!)	100-500 ng/L abnormal but not critical for ventricular strain (mild) Critical RED FLAG: >500 critical for positive correlation of HF exacerbation	*CHF exacerbation *Ventricular hypertrophy (cardiomyopathy) *Severe hypertension	*Aggressive diuresis for fluid overload *May be on NTG gtt or po Nitrates to decrease preload which decreases workload of heart	THINK CARDIAC-HF *Assess respiratory status for tachypnea and breath sounds closely for basilar or scattered crackles *Assess HR and SBP carefully to promote decreased cardiac workload (heart rate <80 and SBP <140 *Assess tolerance to activity closely *Assess I&O closely *Assess K+ closely with loop diuretics

References

1. Van Leeuwen, A. & Poelhuis-Leth, D.J. (2009). *Davis's comprehensive handbook of laboratory and diagnostic tests with nursing implications*. Third ed. Philadelphia, PA: F.A. Davis Company.

Appendix H: Most Commonly Used Categories of Drugs in the Clinical Setting

Category	Class	Body System Impacted	Generic Name	Brand Name	Most Common Side Effects (italics) SEVERE	Nursing Considerations and Vital Assessments
BP Agents	ACE Inhibitors	CV	Captopril Enalapril Lisinopril	Capoten Vasotec Prinivil	*Cough hypotension* **angioedema agranulocytosis**	*Obtain BP before administering-hold typically if SBP <90 *Change position slowly-especially with elderly to prevent orthostatic changes *Monitor for decreased WBC count, hyperkalemia, liver function, and GFR/creatinine (metabolized by liver-excreted by kidneys)
	Beta blockers	CV	Atenolol Metoprolol Propranolol	Tenormin Lopressor Inderal	*Fatigue, weakness,* **bradycardia, CHF, pulmonary edema**	*Obtain BP and HR before administering-hold typically if SBP <90. HR <60 *Change position slowly-especially with elderly to prevent orthostatic changes *Contraindicated in worsening CHF, bradycardia of heart block…use with caution in diabetes, liver disease
	Calcium Channel Blockers	CV	Amlodipine Diltiazem Nifedipine Verapamil	Norvasc Cardizem Procardia Calan	*Peripheral edema,* **Cardiac arrythmias, CHF**	*Obtain BP and HR before administering-hold typically if SBP <90. HR <60 *Change position slowly-especially with elderly to prevent orthostatic changes *Measure I&O closely and fluid status due to potential for edema *Monitor liver and kidney function (metabolized in liver-excreted by kidneys)

Category	Class	Body System Impacted	Generic Name	Brand Name	Most Common Side Effects (italics) SEVERE	Nursing Considerations and Vital Assessments
	Vaso-dilators	CV	Hydralazine Isosorbide Nitroglycerine	Apresoline Isordil Tridil	*Dizziness, headache, hypotension, tachycardia*	*Obtain BP before administering-hold typically if SBP <90 *Tolerance common and serious problem with long acting nitrates. Nitrates lose their effectiveness if transdermal patches remain on continually. Patches must be taken off at night and then reapplied in the morning *Contraindicated if client taking any erectile dysfunction meds as these are a similar nitrate that improves blood circulation to the penis-synergistic effect can cause dramatic hypotension
Cholesterol Binding Agents	Statins	CV	Lovastatin Rosuvastatin Simvastatin Atorvastatin	Mevacor Crestor Zocor Lipitor	*Abd. Cramps, constipation, diarrhea, heartburn, rashes* **Rhabdomyolosis**	*Can cause liver injury/damage-watch ALT/AST/alk phos/bili levels closely *Can cause muscle injury/damage. If CPK elevated DC use
Heart Rhythm Stabilizers	Class III Antiarryth.	CV	Amiodarone	Cordorone	*Dizziness, fatigue, malaise, ataxia, bradycardia* <u>**Pulmonary fibrosis**</u>	*Assess for QT prolongation-can lead to VT/VF with IV administration *Assess HR before giving-hold if <60 with IV administration *Can cause pulmonary toxicity with chronic use-assess for crackles, diminished breath sounds, fatigue, pleuritic chest pain *Assess for neurotoxicity (ataxia, muscle weakness, tingling in fingers/toes, tremors) *Assess for signs of thyroid dysfunction (lethargy, weight gain, edema...HYPOTHYROIDISM or tachycardia, weight loss, nervousness-HYPERTHYROIDISM) *Monitor liver labs (AST-ALT-bili) and throid labs (T3-T4)

Category	Class	Body System Impacted	Generic Name	Brand Name	Most Common Side Effects (italics) SEVERE	Nursing Considerations and Vital Assessments
	Digitalis	CV	Digoxin	Lanoxin	*Fatigue, bradycardia, anorexia, N&V* **arrythmias**	*Assess apical pulse for 1 minute before giving-hold if <60 *Increases fall risk for elderly-assess closely *Monitor K+, Mg+, Ca+ levels closely-if these are low more likely to become dig. toxic. Elderly also more likely to be dig. toxic *Assess serum levels of digoxin (norm 0.5-2.0 ng/ml) ***Assess for toxicity: abd. pain, anorexia, N&V, bradycardia, visual changes**
Diuretics	Loop	CV	Furosemide	Lasix	*Dehydration, hypovolemia, hypokalemia, hyponatremia, hypomagnesemia*	*Obtain BP before administering-hold typically if SBP <90 *Change position slowly-especially with elderly to prevent orthostatic changes *Monitor sodium and K+ levels closely as well as Mg+, GFR and creatinine *assess for signs of hypokalemia (weakness-fatigue-increased PVC's on cardiac monitor). Potassium is the lyte that will be most quickly depleted in most pts
	K+ sparing		Spironolactone	Aldactone	*Hyperkalemia*	*Aldactone and ACE inhibitors can cause resultant hyperkalemia *If on Aldactone-make sure does not use potassium based salt substitutes or foods rich in K+
	Thiazides		Hydrochlorothiazide	HCTZ	*Hypokalemia*	*Monitor BP, I&O, daily weight and for presence of edema ***If on digoxin, assess closely for signs of dig. toxicity since they are at higher risk of developing because of the K+ depleting effects of the diuretic** Monitor K+, Na+, Mg+, and creatinine levels closely

Category	Class	Body System Impacted	Generic Name	Brand Name	Most Common Side Effects (italics) SEVERE	Nursing Considerations and Vital Assessments
Anti-Coagulants	Anti-Coagulant	Blood	Warfarin	Coumadin	**Bleeding (GI) most common**	***Assess for bleeding: tarry black, or maroon stools, nosebleeds, bruising, or hematuria** *Monitor Hgb, INR (therapeutic range is 2-3 for anticoagulation) *Excreted by liver-assess AST/ALT
	Anti-Coagulant		Heparin (IV/SQ) Lovenox (SQ)	Heparin Lovenox	*Anemia, thrombocytopenia* **Bleeding**	* **Assess for bleeding: tarry black, or maroon stools, nosebleeds, bruising, or hematuria** *Administer SQ in abd, NOT proximal to umbilicus *Pinch abd. fold before/during administration *Assess for decreased platelets (heparin induced thrombocytopenia-HIT)
Analgesic	Narcotics	CNS	Hydromorphone Morphine Oxycodone Codeine	Dilaudid MS Contin Oxycontin Codeine	*Confusion, sedation, hypotension, constipation* <u>**Resp. Depression**</u>	*Assess BP-HR-RR and LOC closely after giving-especially when drug is peaking (this will vary on drug and if given po vs. IV-check your drug book!) *Elderly more sensitive to effects of opiod analgesics and develop SE and resp. complications more frequently *THEREFORE always give LOW range if ordered *Assess bowel function closely due to risk of constipation…determine LBM! *Tolerance develops with long-term use-will need higher doses to achieve adequate pain relief
	Combo	CNS	oxycodone-acetaminophen hydrocodone-acetaminophen codeine-acetaminophen	Percocet Vicodin Tylenol #3	*Confusion, sedation, hypotension, constipation* <u>**Resp. Depression**</u>	*Assess pain relief 1 hour (PEAK) after giving po *Assess BP-HR-R and LOC closely after giving-especially when drug is peaking. *Elderly more sensitive to effects of opiod analgesics and develop SE and resp. complications more frequently *THEREFORE always give LOW range if ordered *Assess bowel function closely due to risk of constipation…determine LBM! *Tolerance develops with long-term use-will need higher doses to achieve adequate pain relief

Category	Class	Body System Impacted	Generic Name	Brand Name	Most Common Side Effects (italics)	Nursing Considerations and Vital Assessments
	Non-narcotic	CNS	Acetaminophen Aspirin	Tylenol ASA	**Liver failure, toxicity w/OD or high doses**	*Max. daily dose is 4000 mg. Liver damage can result if reaches this level or is malnourished or abuse of ETOH more likely to be toxic *Monitor liver labs (AST-ALT-bili-PT/INR) with Tylenol & Aspirin *Give Aspirin w/food to minimize risk of ulcer/GI bleed
	Non-steroidal anti-inflammatory (NSAID)	CNS	Ibuprofen Indomethacin Naproxsyn Ketorolac	Motrin/Advil Indocin Aleve Toradol	*Headache, constipation, N&V* **GI Bleeding, Hepatitis**	*Give w/food to minimize risk of ulcer/GI bleed *Assess for GI bleeding: tarry black, or maroon stools, lightheaded, tachycardia *Elderly are at higher risk to develop GI bleeding *Monitor liver labs (AST-ALT-bili-PT/INR) *Assess response to pain med 1 hour after giving *Increases bleeding times. Be sure to DC before surgery. Effects last 24 hours after last dose
Anti-anxiety	Anti-anxiety	CNS	Alprazolam Diazepam Lorazepam	Xanax Valium Ativan	*Dizziness, drowsiness, lethargy*	*Assess closely for dizziness, drowsiness with first doses *CNS side effects increase w/elderly. THEREFORE always give LOW range if ordered
Anti-convulsant	Anti-convulsant	CNS	Carbamazepine Gabapentin Levetiracetam Phenytoin	Tegretol Neurontin Keppra Dilantin	*Drowsiness, ataxia, weakness*	*Neurontin commonly used for neuropathic pain or chronic pain syndromes
Anti-depressant	Selective Serotonin Reuptake Inhibitors (SSRI)	CNS	Citalopram Fluoxetine Paroxetine	Celexa Prozac Paxil	*Drowsiness, headache, insomnia, nervousness, tremor*	*Requires 2 weeks to have physiologic effects when new medication *Assess for increased suicidal tendencies with new therapy
Anti-Parkinson		CNS	Carbidopa-Levodopa	Sinemet	*N&V, involuntary movements*	*OK to give w/food to minimize GI side effects *Assess for Parkinson's effects improving: rigidity, tremors, shuffling gait, drooling

Category	Class	Body System Impacted	Generic Name	Brand Name	Most Common Side Effects (italics) SEVERE	Nursing Considerations and Vital Assessments
	Anti-psychotic	CNS	Quetiapine Haloperidol	Seroquel Haldol	*Constipation, dry mouth, blurred vision, extrapyramidal reactions (EPSE)*	*OK to give w/food to minimize GI irritation *Assess mental status (mood-orientation-behavior) before and after giving *Expected effect is DECREASED agitation/restlessness if given prn *Monitor for increased restlessness-agitation after first dose. This is a side effect *Monitor for EPSE-these are Parkinson like: difficulty/speaking or swallowing, loss of balance, pill rolling, rigidity, shuffling gait and tremors *Monitor for dystonic reaction: muscle spasm, especially in neck causing head to stay fixed on affected side, weakness of extremities
Gastric Acid Reducers	Proton Pump Inhibitors (PPI)	GI	Pantoprazole Omeprazole	Protonix Prilosec	*Abdominal pain*	*May give w/without regards to food *Assess frequently for epigastric/abd pain and blood in stool, emesis
	Histamine Blockers (H2)	GI	Cimetadine Famotidine Ranitidine	Tagamet Pepcid Zantec	*Confusion,* <u>**Arrythmias**</u>	*Administer w/food to prolong effects *Assess frequently for epigastric/abd pain and blood in stool, emesis. Given to prevent ulcers. This would be indicative of GI bleeding
Anti-Nausea		GI	Ondansetron Prochlorperazine Promethazine	Zofran Compazine Phenergan	*Headache, constipation, diarrhea, extrapyramidal reactions (Compazine only)*	*With prochlorperazine (Compazine) monitor for sedation and dystonic reaction: muscle spasm, especially in neck causing head to stay fixed on affected side, weakness of extremities *May develop EPSE w/prochlorperazine. Assess for difficulty/speaking or swallowing, loss of balance, pill rolling, rigidity, shuffling gait and tremors
Laxatives		GI	Docusate Sennosides Psyllium	Colace Senokot Metamucil	*Abd cramps, diarrhea*	* Assess GI system carefully for abd distention, presence of bowel sounds, and color, consistency and amount of stool *Hold if has recent pattern of loose stools

Category	Class	Body System Impacted	Generic Name	Brand Name	Most Common Side Effects (italics) **SEVERE**	Nursing Considerations and Vital Assessments
	Bronchial dilators	Resp.	Albuterol Albuterol-ipatropium	Ventolin Combivent	*Nervousness, restlessness, tremor, chest pain, palpitations*	*Assess breath sounds, pulse and BP before and after giving. Note amount, color and character of any sputum *Inhaled albuterol onsets in 5-15" and peaks in 1 hour *Assess therapeutic benefit of neb in 15"
	Broncho Dilator & Steroid Combo	Resp.	Fluticasone-salmeterol	Advair	*Headache, nervousness*	*Assess breath sounds before and after giving. Note amount, color and character of any sputum *Because it is a maintenance combination, will not likely see any changes after administration *Rinse mouth with water after use to prevent thrush
	Inhaled Steroids	Resp.	Triamcinalone Fluticasone	Azmacort Flovent	*Headache, pharyngitis, flu like symptoms*	*Monitor resp. status and breath sounds closely *May cause increased serum and urine glucose levels due to steroid effect-monitor as needed
Anti-Infectives	Anti-fungal	Systemic	Fluconazole Nystatin	Diflucan Mycostatin	**Liver toxicity**	*Obtain any specimen cultures before giving first dose *Excreted by kidneys so monitor renal function (creatinine) closely
	Cephalosporin	Systemic	Cephalexin	Keflex	*Diarrhea* **Colitis, seizures**	*Obtain any specimen cultures before giving first dose *Can give w/wo food *Assess for allergic response of any kind (rash-itching-hives-anaphylactic-resp. distress) *Determine if has allergy to penicillin, give w/caution as there is risk for cross sensitivity to penicillin *Continue to assess for response to infection (temp-appearance of wound-WBC/neutrophils)
	Penicillins	Systemic	Amoxicillin Ampicillin	Amoxil Polycillin	*Rashes, diarrhea* **Seizures, allergic reactions, colitis**	*obtain any specimen cultures before giving first dose but do need results *can give w/wo food *assess for allergic response of any kind (rash-itching-hives-anaphylactic-resp. distress) *determine if has allergy to cephalosporins, give w/caution as there is risk for cross sensitivity to cephalosporins *continue to assess for response to infection

Category	Class	Body System Impacted	Generic Name	Brand Name	Most Common Side Effects (italics) SEVERE	Nursing Considerations and Vital Assessments
	Sulfonamides	Systemic	Sulfamethoxazole & trimethoprim	Bactrim	*Epigastric pain, N&V, itching, rash*	*Obtain any specimen cultures before giving first dose *Give on empty stomach with full glass of water *Primarily used for urinary tract infection-assess response (fever-ongoing painful/burning urination) *Assess for allergic response of any kind (rash-itching-hives-anaphylactic-resp. distress)
	Tetracyclines	Systemic	Doxycycline Tetracycline	Doxy Tetracyn	*Diarrhea, N&V, light sensitivity*	*Obtain any specimen cultures before giving first dose *Give on empty stomach with full glass of water *Assess for allergic response of any kind (rash-itching-hives-anaphylactic-resp. distress)
Steroids		Systemic	Dexamethasone Hydrocortisone Prednisone	Decadron Solu-cortef Deltasone	*Depression, hypertension, anorexia, nausea, bruising*	*Give orally w/meals to avoid GI irritation *Causes hyperglycemia-monitor glucose levels closely especially if diabetic *Decreases immune response and WBC count: assess closely for signs of infection *Decreases serum K+ levels and increases Na+. Monitor these labs closely *Assess for signs of adrenal insufficiency that can cause hypotension, weight loss, weakness, N&V, confusion, peripheral edema *Monitor I&O and daily weights for these reasons
Thyroid Hormone		Systemic	Levothyroxine	Synthroid	*Usually seen only when excessive doses cause hyperthyroid symptoms*	*give on empty stomach in the morning *assess apical pulse and BP prior to giving periodically *monitor thyroid function tests (T3-T4-TSH)
Musculo-skeletal Agents	Arthritis	Joints	Leflunomide	Cerebrex	*Dizziness, drowsiness, rash, ataxia*	*assess range of motion and degree of swelling and pain in affected joint
	Gout			Alloprim Colchicine	*Rash-Allopurinol Diarrhea, N&V-colchicine*	*give with meals to minimize gastric irritation *monitor for joint pain and swelling

Category	Class	Body System Impacted	Generic Name	Brand Name	Most Common Side Effects (italics) **SEVERE**	Nursing Considerations and Vital Assessments
	Muscle relaxants	Muscle	Cyclobenzaprine methocarbamol	Flexeril Robaxin	*Dizziness, drowsiness, dry mouth,*	*Assess for pain, muscle stiffness and range of motion before and periodically throughout therapy *Monitor elderly closely for increased sedation and weakness *Administer with caution in combination w/narcotics due to increased sedation with any age
	Electrolyte replacement	Systemic	Potassium Chloride	K-dur	*Abd. Pain, N&V, diarrhea* **Arrythmias (PVC's or V-Tach)**	*Administer w/meals-is very hard on stomach! *Monitor serum K+ closely throughout therapy *Assess for signs of hypokalemia (weakness-fatigue-increased PVC's on cardiac monitor) *Assess for signs of hyperkalemia (bradycardia-fatigue-muscle weakness-confusion)

References

1. Vallerand, A.H., Sanoski, C.A., & Deglin, J.H. (2013) *Davis's drug guide for nurses*. Thirteenth ed. Philadelphia, PA: F.A. Davis Company.

Appendix I

Comprehending Cardiac Medications:
Foundational Cardiac Concepts That Must Be Understood

Cardiac Output (CO) …CO=SVxHR (stroke volume x heart rate)
- **Cardiac output:** The amount of blood the heart pumps through the circulatory system in a minute. The amount of blood put out by the left ventricle of the heart in one contraction is called the stroke volume. The stroke volume and the heart rate determine the cardiac output. A normal adult has a cardiac output of 4.7 liters (5 quarts) of blood per minute (normal range 4–8 liters/minute).
- **Stroke volume:** Stroke volume (SV) is the volume of blood pumped from one ventricle of the heart with each beat. The term stroke volume can apply to each of the two ventricles of the heart, although it usually refers to the left ventricle. The stroke volumes for each ventricle are generally equal, both being approximately 70 mL in most adults.
- Stroke volume is influenced by the amount of blood that returns to right atrium from venous circulation (RIGHT SIDE) and left atrium (LEFT SIDE) from pulmonary veins.
    - Higher SV increases workload of the heart…typically due to too much VOLUME.
    - Tachycardia INCREASES cardiac O2 demands, workload, and DECREASES stroke volume because there is less time for the ventricles to fill.
    - Goal of medication therapy with any cardiac patient is to DECREASE cardiac workload through manipulating SV, HR, preload, afterload, and contractility.

Preload
Preload is the filling pressure of the right ventricle (RV) and left ventricle (LV). It is influenced by how full the body's tank is and amount of venous return. Higher venous return (fluid volume overload) will result in higher SV. Fluid volume deficit will result in lower SV. If monitored with a central venous line, normal values are 2–6 mm/Hg. This is also the same as a central venous pressure (CVP).
- Pressure/Stretch in ventricles end diastole just before contraction.
- In a healthy heart, as you increase preload, you will increase stroke volume which will increase force of contraction (Starlings law).
- Only up to a certain point will this continue, then further stretching may actually decrease contractility. This is what will happen with patients with chronic heart failure.
- Drugs that cause venous dilation (nitrates)-DECREASE preload.
- Diuretics that eliminate excess fluid volume DECREASE preload.

Starling's Law of the Heart:
- If preload is increased, greater quantity of blood that is ejected during systole due to increased stretch of the myocardium and larger amount of circulating blood volume present.
- But only up to a maximal point. Greatest force of contraction is when the muscle fibers are stretched 2 ½ times their normal length.
- Overstretch of cardiac muscle is like an overstretched rubber band; it will DECREASE cardiac contractility and efficiency over time. This is why an enlarged heart due to heart failure is NOT a good thing!

Afterload
- Force of resistance that the LV must generate to open aortic valve.
- Correlates w/SBP–How much pressure is needed to push blood out of the LV, and into systemic arterial circulation.
- Influenced by resistance of blood vessels in the body–Are the arteries dilated or constricted? If arterial vasodilation is present, afterload is DECREASED and workload of the heart is DECREASED. If arterial vasoconstriction is present, afterload is INCREASED and workload of the heart is INCREASED.
- Arterial vasodilators (Ca++ channel blockers [CCB], ACE inhibitors) then DECREASE afterload and decrease the workload of the heart.

3) Contractility: Contractility of the cardiac myocardium independent of Starling mechanism
- Ability of heart to change force of inherent contraction strength as needed.
- Influenced by Ca++ in action potential…Therefore, how will calcium channel blockers (CCB) influence contractility? (They will DECREASE contractility and must be used with caution in those with heart failure).
- Decrease in contractility (inotropic effect) DECREASES cardiac workload and O2 demands.
- Negative inotropic meds: CCB, beta blockers
- Positive inotropic: Digoxin, Dopamine & Epinephrine gtts.

Ejection Fraction–% (EF) on echocardiogram
- 60–70% normal.
- With each contraction 60–70% of the blood in the LV is ejected into circulation.
- As this percent goes down, it is reflecting the loss of cardiac contractility and degree of heart failure.
- 30–35% EF is half normal cardiac output.
- 10–15% EF end-stage heart failure-terminal.

I. Angiotensin Converting Enzyme (ACE) Inhibitors...(end in "pril")
- Captopril (Capoten)
- Enalapril (Vasotec)
- Lisinopril (Prinivil)

Mechanism of Action: A plasma protein-renin is secreted by the kidneys when BP falls. This converts inactive liver protein angiotensinogen to angiotensin I. The conversion to angiotensin II is enhanced by angiotensin-converting-enzymes (ACE) from the lungs to be one of the most potent vasoconstrictors in the body. The effects of angiotensin II are:
- Vasoconstriction of arterioles and veins (increases afterload).
- Stimulation of the sympathetic nervous system (SNS) (increases workload of heart).
- Retention of water by the kidneys due to aldosterone a hormone secreted by the adrenal glands (increases preload).

In heart failure (HF), each of these normal physiologic actions will worsen underlying HF and must be counteracted. This is why ACE-I are the first medication used in HF.
ACE inhibitors block the conversion of angiotensin I to angiotensin II. This inhibition decreases angiotensin II concentrations and causes:
- Vasodilation which decreases SBP (decreases afterload) and decreases sodium and water retention (decreases preload).

Uses: HTN, HF, coronary artery disease (CAD)

Side Effects–Most Common: hypotension, dry cough, dizziness
- Angioedema (life threatening) Laryngeal swelling that can cause asphyxia. Facial swelling also concerning precursor and a clinical RED FLAG.

Nursing Considerations:
- Obtain BP before administering–hold typically if SBP <90.
- Change position slowly–especially with elderly to prevent orthostatic changes.
- Monitor for decreased WBC count, hyperkalemia as well as liver function, and creatinine (metabolized by liver-excreted by kidneys).

II. Beta Blockers...(end in "lol")
- Metoprolol (Lopressor)
- Atenolol (Tenormin)
- Propranolol (Inderal)
- Labetolol (Trandate)

Mechanism of Action: Selectively inhibits beta (sympathetic/fight or flight) receptors primarily of the heart (Beta 1). Sympathetic nervous system (SNS) stimulation normally causes:
- Increased heart rate.
- Increased BP.
- Increase myocardium contractility and oxygen demand.
- ALL THESE EFFECTS INCREASE WORKLOAD OF THE HEART!

By blocking the SNS it effectively causes the opposite effects and DECREASES workload of the heart...decreased heart rate, decreased BP, and decreased contractility. This is why it must be used with caution in those with history of HF. They have excessive activation of SNS which will worsen CHF over time. B-Blockers very effective to manage this complication of HF, and will commonly be used in addition to ACE-I.

Uses: HTN, HF, acute MI, CAD, ventricular dysrhythmias

Side Effects–Most Common: bradycardia, hypotension, fatigue, weakness

Nursing Considerations:
- Obtain BP and HR before administering–hold typically if SBP <90. HR <60.
- Change position slowly–especially with elderly to prevent orthostatic changes.
- Contraindicated in worsening HF, bradycardia, heart block...use with caution in diabetes, liver disease (1)

III. Calcium Channel Blockers
- Diltiazem (Cardizem)
- Verapamil (Calan)
- Nifedipine (Procardia)
- Amlodipine (Norvasc)

Mechanism of Action: Inhibits or "blocks" the influx of extracellular calcium into the membranes of the heart and vascular smooth muscle cells of heart and body. This blocking of calcium ions is responsible for causing the following:
- Dilation of coronary and systemic arteries w/resultant decrease in BP (improves cardiac 02 supply & decreases afterload).
- Decrease of myocardium contractility (decreases workload).
- Slows AV node conduction (decreases heart rate).
- Diltiazem most commonly used to slow HR and AV node conduction in atrial fibrillation.

Uses: HTN, angina, controlling rapid heart rate in SVT or atrial fibrillation.

Side Effects–Most Common: peripheral edema, hypotension, constipation.

Nursing Considerations:
- Change position slowly–especially with elderly to prevent orthostatic changes.
- Measure I&O closely and fluid status due to potential for edema.
- Monitor liver and kidney function (metabolized in liver-excreted by kidneys).
- Obtain BP and HR before administering–hold typically if SBP <90. HR <60 (1).

IV. Nitrates
- Nitroglycerine subl. (Nitrostat)–SHORT acting
- Isosorbide Mononitrate (Imdur)–LONG acting
- Isosorbide Dinitrate (Isordil)–LONG acting
- Nitrodur topical patches–LONG acting

Mechanism of Action: Able to relax and dilate both coronary arterial vessels and systemic venous smooth muscle.
- Dilation of veins reduces amount of blood that returns to heart (decreases preload). With less blood to pump, cardiac output is reduced and workload of the heart decreased lowering myocardial oxygen demand.
- Dilation of coronary arteries can help improve blood flow to heart as well as well as relieve angina caused by coronary artery vasospasm.

Uses: Angina

Side Effects–Most Common: hypotension, tachycardia, dizziness, headache (dilates cerebral vessels causing mini migraine)

Nursing Considerations:
- Tolerance common and serious problem with long acting nitrates. Nitrates lose their effectiveness if transdermal patches remain on continually. Patches must be taken off. at night and then reapplied in the morning.
- Contraindicated if client taking any erectile dysfunction meds as these are a similar nitrate that improves blood circulation to the penis–synergistic effect can cause dramatic hypotension (1).

V. Diuretics
- Furosemide (Lasix) -most potent
- Bumetanide (Bumex) -most potent
- Hydrochlorathiazide (HCTZ)-mod. potency

- Spirinolactone (Aldactone)-mild potency-K+ sparing

Mechanism of Action:
- **Loop diuretics**–Most potent diuretics that prevent sodium reabsorption in the loop of henle causing rapid/large diuresis with resultant loss of K+, and smaller amounts of Mg+, and Na+. Because of their potency are not used for maintenance but when large diuresis is desired such as in acute HF exacerbation (decreases preload).

- **Thiazide diuretics**–Increases excretion of sodium and water by inhibiting sodium reabsorption in distal tubule. Most common maintenance diuretic. K+ loss needs to be monitored.

- **Potassium sparing diuretics**–Weakest of all diuretics due to not blocking reabsorption of sodium. Used when client is at risk for developing hypokalemia. Must also assess for development of hyperkalemia.

Uses: HTN, HF, renal insufficiency/acute renal failure

Side Effects–Most Common: dehydration, orthostatic hypotension, hypokalemia, hyponatremia, hypomagnesemia with loop and thiazide diuretics, potential for hyperkalemia w/spironolactone (Aldactone).

Nursing Considerations: *Change position slowly-especially with elderly to prevent orthostatic changes.
- Change position slowly-especially with elderly to prevent orthostatic changes.
- Obtain BP before administering–hold typically if SBP <90.
- Monitor sodium and K+ levels closely as well as GFR and creatinine.
- Aldactone and ACE inhibitors can cause resultant hyperkalemia.
- If on Aldactone–make sure does not use potassium based salt substitutes or foods rich in K+ (1).

Appendix J

Clinical Reasoning Questions to Develop Nurse Thinking
(Formulate and reflect before and after report, but BEFORE seeing patient the first time)

1. What is the primary problem and what is the underlying cause/pathophysiology of this problem?

2. What clinical data from the chart is RELEVANT and needs to be trended because it is clinically significant?

3. What nursing priority will guide your plan of care?

4. What nursing interventions will you initiate based on this priority and what are the desired outcomes?

5. What body system(s) will you focus on based on your patient's primary problem or nursing care priority?

6. What is the worst possible/most likely complication(s) to anticipate based on the primary problem?

7. What nursing assessments will you need to initiate to identify this complication if it develops?

While Providing Care...*(Review and note during shift after initial patient assessment)*

8. What clinical assessment data did you just collect that is RELEVANT and needs to be TRENDED because it is clinically significant to detect a change in status?

9. Does your nursing priority or plan of care need to be modified in any way after assessing your patient?

10. After reviewing the primary care providers note, what is the rationale for any new orders or changes made?

11. What educational/discharge priorities have you identified and how will you address them?

Caring and the "Art" of Nursing

12. What is the patient likely experiencing/feeling right now in this situation?

13. What can I do to engage myself with this patient's experience, and show that he/she matters to me as a person?

Appendix K

Clinical Reasoning Resources and KeithRN

Though my website was originally built and designed to meet the needs of nurse educators, it also contains many resources for students or new nurses that will promote thinking like a nurse and build on the content of this book. In addition to the three levels of case studies that were discussed in chapter 5, I have numerous resources, all FREE downloads on the following tabs that may be helpful to promote your learning as a student, graduate nurse or even as a nurse educator!

KeithRN Tabs

- **Clinical Resources**

  In addition to the handouts and worksheets that are included in the appendices of this book, there are other clinical resources that I want to highlight under this tab:

  - *Alternative Clinical Assignment* (under "Clinical Reasoning" sub-tab)
    - ✓ If you are a nurse educator, this is something you must check out if you have too many students in the clinical setting and need an alternative assignment. This takes an entire clinical time of 4-6 hours to complete and best if done with another student. A nursing assessment is incorporated into this assignment, but it does NOT involve patient care. Situates clinical reasoning and needed nurse thinking!

  - *Medication Prep Worksheet*
    - ✓ This is a different format from what is found in this book. See which one you prefer!

  - *Lab Values Prep Worksheet*
    - ✓ This is a different format from what is found in this book. See which one you prefer!

- **Classroom Resources**
  - I have posted all of my PowerPoint presentations that I have created as a nurse educator in the original doc. file. They are organized by body system and the topics under that body system. I have extensive notes for each of the slides. If you print up the PowerPoint in "notes" you will have them to supplement your learning. I had to remove all illustrations for copyright purposes, so they do not have a "pop" factor, but the content and notes are worth checking out!

- **Teaching Caring**
  - This tab will be of interest to the nurse educator if you desire to intentionally situate caring and caring behaviors in the clinical setting. You can build on my adaptation of Kristen Swanson's theory of caring that is described in chapter 1 in my book. Check out the content and downloads that can help you intentionalize caring in your clinical!

- **Medical Missions**

    Though appendix L goes into further detail on this topic, there are three links that are worth highlighting here that are found under the sub-tab "Medical Mission Essentials".

    - *Practical Preparation*
        - ✓ Three handouts that will practically prepare you for a medical missions trip. This includes raising financial support, covering all the details before you leave, and transitioning after you return. This information will help make your medical mission trip a blessing to you and others!

    - *Medications and Medical Supplies*
        - ✓ I have personally compiled this list of the most common medications and medical supplies that are needed to treat most clinical presentations in an outpatient community health outreach when I was in Haiti. This list will lay a solid foundation that can be easily modified to meet your needs in the country you are serving.

    - *Christian Ministry Resources*
        - ✓ If you or your team have a desire to minister not only to the physical needs but also to the spiritual needs, this short list will provide links to resources to effectively communicate God's love.

- **YouTube Channel: Think Like a Nurse**
    - I have a wide range of short videos that build on many of the topics in this book and med/surg topics such as sepsis. I am adding new videos regularly so check back frequently or better yet, subscribe to this channel!

Appendix L

Medical Missions and Faith Based Resources

To put the needs of the developing world in context, if 100 jetliners crashed today killing 26,500 people it would get your and the world's attention. If this happened day after day you would demand that something be done to stop this ongoing loss of precious human life! But a tragedy of this scope occurs every day in the developing world. **26,500 children die** of preventable causes related to their poverty **every day.** Over one year this equates to 10,000,000 lives lost every year (1).

After the massive earthquake struck Haiti in January, 2010, I felt powerless and helpless yet wanted to do something to help with my ED background. The news reports dramatically witnessed the urgency of the medical needs of so many thousands dead and wounded with minimal resources to care for the suffering. I was finally able to go as part of a medical mission team through our church in May, 2010. Though the critically wounded were by then cared for, our team was able to provide much-needed routine clinic care for many living in the tent cities in Port au Prince. Once we left Haiti after a week, there was no coordination of other health care providers to take our place.

I have been back twice since then, most recently with a team comprised of my second-year nursing students who were forever changed by their ability to make a difference in the developing world where the needs are great and ongoing. I have a photo gallery of one of our trips as a team on my home page of KeithRN. A picture truly is worth a thousand words! Though our team accomplishments may seem small and a proverbial "drop in the bucket," the "drop" matters, because every person matters to God and each of us have equal worth as we are created in His image.

Haiti has the highest rates of infant, under-age-5, and maternal in the Western Hemisphere. The infant mortality rate is **57** per thousand in 2007; in the US it is **6.7** deaths per 1,000. Maternal mortality is **523** deaths per 100,000 births in Haiti, compared with **13** per 100,000 in the US. Diarrhea, respiratory infections, malaria, tuberculosis, and HIV/AIDS are the leading causes of death. Not coincidentally, Haiti has the lowest number of nurses/1000 population in the world: 0.11 nurses/1000. Though we lament the nursing shortage here in the US (16th in the world at 9.37/1000), nothing compares to this! As a nurse, you now have a skill that can serve others wherever you choose to practice. Based on my own personal observations and the feedback and reflections of my nursing students, even a one-week service trip can minister to the needs of the poor, possibly save a life, and give you a new lens to see the world by.

One book that continually challenges me is *Don't Waste Your Life* by John Piper. Each one of us has a finite amount of time to live our life for what really matters. The greatest tragedy is to come to the end of your days realizing that you wasted the one life you have been given on this earth. In addition to not wasting my life, I also do not want to waste this opportunity to encourage anyone who is reading this book to impact those in the developing world with a variety of ways to serve.

If you are a student who has textbooks you know you will never open after graduation, or an educator who has older editions of textbooks gathering dust, SEND THEM TO ME! I have contacts in Liberia, an English-speaking African country that is in desperate need to have such basic resources as nursing textbooks because of the devastation to the country and its resources after a prolonged civil war. It is not uncommon to have an entire nursing class of eighty students have just a few textbooks that are shared by all.

I have a vision to not just do for those in need but to improve nursing education in the developing world. I also have a vision to teach/train native community health workers who could safely provide basic clinic level care as a mission and outreach of the local church. If you have an interest to serve in this capacity and help make this vision possible, please contact me. I have also listed organizations that specialize in short-term medical mission outreach in the developing world. I also have a Medical Missions tab on my website that has numerous resources for those who may be interested in serving in this context as well.

Medical Mission Resources:

- Bulk Medications for Medical Ministry: Blessings International: http://www.blessing.org/
- Medical Mission Outreach: Medical Teams International http://www.medicalteams.org/Home.aspx
- Medical Mission Outreach: Global Health Outreach
- Nursing Education: Haiti Nursing Foundation: http://haitinursing.org/
- Book: *When Helping Hurts: Alleviating Poverty Without Hurting the Poor...and Yourself* by Steve Corbett & Brian Fikkert
- Book: *Don't Waste Your Life* by John Piper

Faith Based Resources

- Book: *Called to Care: A Christian Worldview for Nursing* by Judith Allen Shelly & Arlene B. Miller
- Book: *The Nurse with an Alabaster Jar: A Biblical Approach to Nursing* by Mary Elizabeth O'Brien & Judith Allen Shelly
- Journal: Journal of Christian Nursing (JCN)
    - iPad app...FREE download of JCN for limited trial
- Website: Nurses Christian Fellowship: http://ncf-jcn.org/

References

Preface
1. Eldredge, J. (2001). *Wild at heart: Discovering the secret of a man's soul.* Nashville, TN: Thomas Nelson.
2. Benner, P., Sutphen, M., Leonard, V., & Day, L. (2010). *Educating nurses: A call for radical transformation.* San Francisco, CA: Jossey-Bass.

Introduction
1. Cho, J., Laschinger, H.K.S., & Wong, C. (2006). Workplace empowerment, work engagement and organizational commitment of new graduate nurses, *Nursing Leadership, 19*(3), 43-62.
2. Clark, C.M., & Springer, P.J. (2012). Nurse residents' firsthand accounts on transition to practice. *Nursing Outlook, 60*(4), E2-E8.

Chapter 1: Foundation: The "Art" of Nursing
1. Leininger, M. (1988). Leininger's theory of nursing: Cultural care diversity and university. *Nursing Science Quarterly, 1*, 152-160.
2. Leininger, M. (1991). *Culture care diversity and universality: A theory of nursing.* New York, NY: National League for Nursing.
3. Hampton Robb, E. (1900). *Nursing ethics.* Cleveland, OH: E.C. Koeckert.
4. Benner, P., personal communication, August 10, 2013.
5. Benner, P., & Wrubel, J. (1989). *Primacy of caring: Stress and coping in health and illness.* Menlo Park, CA: Addison-Wesley Publishing Company.
6. Swanson, K.M., (1999). *What is known about caring in nursing: A literary meta-analysis.* In A.S. Hinshaw, S.L. Feetham, & J.L.F. Shaver eds. Handbook of clinical nursing research, Thousand Oaks, CA: Sage Publications.
7. Pre-Licensure KSAS. *QSEN*.com. Retrieved from http://qsen.org/competencies/pre-licensure-ksas/#patient-centered_care
8. Swanson, K.M, (1991). Empirical development of a middle range theory of caring. *Nursing Research, 40*(3), 161-166.
9. Kolcaba, K. (2003). *Comfort Theory and Practice.* New York, NY: Springer.
10. Wilkinson, J.M., & Treas, L.S. (2011). *Fundamentals of nursing,* (2nd ed.). Philadelphia, PA: F.A. Davis Company.
11. McDonald, L. (1999). Nightingale's spirituality: The faith of Florence nightingale. *uoguelph*.ca. Retrieved June 15, 2013 from http://www.uoguelph.ca/~cwfn/spirituality/spirituality.html.
12. Macrae, J. (1995). Nightingale's spiritual philosophy and its significance for modern nursing, *Image Journal of Nursing Scholarship, 27*(8).
13. Lewis Coakley, M. (1990). The faith behind the famous: Florence Nightingale: Christian history sampler. *Christianitytoday*.com. Retrieved from http://www.christianitytoday.com/ch/1990/issue25/2537.html?start=1
14. Benner, P., Hooper-Kyriakidis, P., & Stannard, D.(2011). *Clinical wisdom and interventions in Acute and Critical Care: A thinking-in-action approach.*(2nd ed.). New York, NY: Springer.
15. Benner, P. (2012). International Nurses Christian Fellowship speech.
16. Murphy, L.S., & Walker, M.S. (2013). Spirit-guided care: Christian nursing for the whole person, *Journal of Christian Nursing, 30*(3), 144-152.
17. Rex-Smith, A. (2007). Something more than presence. *Journal of Christian Nursing, 24*(2), 82-87.
18. Faas, A.I. (2004). The intimacy of dying: An act of presence. *Dimensions of Critical Care Nursing, 23*(1), 76-78.

19. Cavendish, R., Konecny, L., Mitzeliotis, C., Russo, D., Kraynyak, B., L., Lanza, M., et al. (2003). Spiritual care activities of nurses using nursing interventions classifications (NIC) labels. *International Journal of Nursing Terminology Classifications, 16,* 120-121.
20. Nurses Christian Fellowship Spiritual Care Guide. *NCF-jcn*.org. Retrieved from http://ncf-jcn.org/sites/ncf/files/uploaded/outreach/spiritualcarecard.pdf
21. Managers note less professionalism among nurses (2013). *Bold Voices, 5*(7), 6.
22. American Nurses Association, (2001). *Code of ethics for nurses with interpretive statements,* Washington, DC, author.

Chapter 2: The Walls: Applied Sciences
1. Pre-Licensure KSAS. *QSEN*.com. Retrieved from http://qsen.org/competencies/pre-licensure-ksas/#patient-centered_care
2. Van Leeuwen, A. & Poelhuis-Leth, D.J. (2009). *Davis's comprehensive handbook of laboratory and diagnostic tests with nursing implications.* (3rd ed.). Philadelphia, PA: F.A. Davis Company.

Chapter 3: The Roof: Thinking like a Nurse
1. Del Bueno, D. (2005). A crisis in critical thinking, *Nursing Education Perspectives, 26*(5), 278-282.
2. Porter-O'Grady, T. (2010). Nurses as knowledge workers. In L. Caputi, *Teaching nursing: The art and science, Vol.2.* Glen Ellyn, IL: College of DuPage Press.
3. Benner, P., Hooper-Kyriakidis, P. & Stannard, D. (2011). *Clinical wisdom and interventions in Acute and Critical Care: A thinking-in-action approach.*(2nd). New York, NY: Springer.
4. Benner, P., Sutphen, M., Leonard, V., & Day, L. (2010). *Educating nurses: A call for radical transformation.* San Francisco, CA: Jossey-Bass.
5. Kothari, R.U., Pancioli, A., Liu, T., Brott, T., & Broderick, J. (1999) Cincinnati prehospital stroke scale: Reproducibility and validity, *Annals of Emergency Medicine, 33,* 373-8.
6. Warning Signs of Stroke. *Stroke*.org. Retrieved June 4, 2013 from http://www.stroke.org/site/PageServer?pagename=symp

Chapter 4: Supporting Structures: Safety, Education & Expert Practice
1. Pre-Licensure KSAS. *QSEN*.com. Retrieved from http://qsen.org/competencies/pre-licensure-ksas/#patient-centered_care
2. Porter-O'Grady, T. (2010). Nurses as knowledge workers. In L. Caputi, *Teaching nursing: The art and science, Vol.2.* Glen Ellyn, IL: College of DuPage Press.
3. Freda, M. (2004) Issues in patient education, *Journal of Midwifery & Woman's Health*, retrieved May 5, 2013 from http://www.medscape.com/viewarticle/478283_3
4. Benner, P. (1982). From novice to expert, *American Journal of Nursing, 82*(3), 402-407.
5. Benner, P., Hooper-Kyriakidis, P., & Stannard, D.(2011). *Clinical wisdom and interventions in Acute and Critical Care: A thinking-in-action approach.*(2nd ed.). New York, NY: Springer.
6. Benner, P., & Wrubel, J. (1989). *Primacy of caring: Stress and coping in health and illness.* Menlo Park, CA: Addison-Wesley Publishing Company.

Appendix A: Skeletons in the Closet: Nurse-to-Nurse Bullying and Incivility
1. Cooper, B. & Curzio, J. (2012). Peer bullying in a pre-registration student nursing population, *Nurse Education Today, 32,* 939-944.
2. Bartholomew, K., (2006), *Ending nurse to nurse hostility: Why nurses eat their young and each other.* Marblehead, MA: HCPro Incorporated.
3. Clark, C. (2013). *Creating and sustaining civility in nursing education,* Indianapolis, IN: Sigma Theta Tau International Publishing.

4. Clark, C.M. (2013). National study on faculty-to-faculty incivility: Strategies to foster collegiality and civility, *Nurse Educator, 38*(3), 98-102.
5. Dellasega, C.A. (2009). Bullying among nurses, *American Journal of Nursing, 109*, 52-58.
6. Johnson, S.J. & Rea, R.E. (2009). Workplace bullying: Concerns for nurse leaders, *The Journal of Nursing Administration, 39*(2), 84-90.
7. Szutenbach, M. (2013). Bullying in nursing: Roots, rationales, and remedies, *Journal of Christian Nursing, 30*(1), 16-23.
8. Murray, J.S. (2008). No more nurse abuse, *American Nurse Today,* 17-19.
9. Incivility in Nursing, NCBON.org. Retrieved from https://docs.google.com/viewer?a=v&q=cache:Z8DGQFYWcZcJ:www.ncbon.com/WorkArea/linkit.aspx%3FLinkIdentifier%3Did%26ItemID%3D2880+how+does+incivility+influence+patient+care&hl=en&gl=us&pid=bl&srcid=ADGEESiJo8QO9zl1fbI2ebfwfG0ypVLSr_1fNxepoJ_dy23E9m3EhQJMGHCDdhBV7tmgQjvpeuYE12JzHQtinZO9aGvIoYQdDVOqVMn9rmYbDH46U0ElDMFQOGEjnSDHu1pQq9aQPUJ9&sig=AHIEtbSTCn4iELvBIRrK69FUvzFx_oExZA
10. Coursey, J.H., Rodriguez, R.E., Dieckmann, L.S., & Austin, P.N. (2013). Successful implementation of policies addressing lateral violence, *AORN Journal, 97*(3), 101-109.
11. Stagg, S.J., Sheridan, D., Jones, R., & Gabel Speroni, K. (2011). Evaluation of a workplace bullying cognitive rehearsal program in a hospital setting, *The Journal of Continuing Education, 12*(9), 395-401.
12. Griffin, M. (2004). Teaching cognitive rehearsal as a shield for lateral violence: An intervention for newly licensed nurses, *The Journal of Continuing Education in Nursing, 35*, 257-263.
13. Pre-Licensure KSAS. QSEN.com. Retrieved from http://qsen.org/competencies/pre-licensure-ksas/#patient-centered_care
14. Clark, C.M. (2008). The dance of incivility in nursing education as described by nursing faculty and students, *Advances in Nursing Science, 31*, E37-E54.
15. Clark, C.M. & Springer, P.J. (2010). Academic nurse leaders' role in fostering a culture of civility in nursing education, *Journal of Nursing Education, 49*(6), 319-325.
16. Clark, C. Cindy's 'Five RITES' for fostering student-driven civility. *reflectionsonnursingleadership*.org. Retrieved from http://www.reflectionsonnursingleadership.org/Pages/Vol39_1_Clark_5RITES.aspx
17. Heinrich, K.T. (2010). An optimist's guide for cultivating civility among academic nurses, *Journal of Professional Nursing, 26*(6), 325-331.
18. Clark, C.M. (2011). Pursuing a culture of civility: An intervention study of one program of nursing, *Nurse Educator, 36*(3), 98-102.
19. Clark, C.M., Olender, L., Kenski, D., & Cardoni, C. (2013). Exploring and addressing faculty-to-faculty incivility: A national perspective and literature review, *Journal of Nursing Education, 52*(4), 211-218.
20. Lester, J. (2009). Not your child's playground: Workplace bullying among community college faculty, *Community College Journal of Research and Practice, 33*, 444-462.
21. (2012, August 6). Nursing Shortage Fact Sheet. AACN.nche.edu. Retrieved from http://www.aacn.nche.edu/media-relations/NrsgShortageFS.pdf
22. (2012, October 24). Nursing Faculty Shortage Fact Sheet. AACN.nche.edu. Retrieved from http://www.aacn.nche.edu/media-relations/FacultyShortageFS.pdf
23. Clark, C.M. & Carnosso, J. (2008). Civility: A concept analysis. *Journal of Theory Construction & Testing, 12*, 11-15.

Appendix B: Skeletons in the Closet: Men in Nursing
1. Meadus, R.J. & Creina Twomey, J. (2011). Men student nurses: The nursing education experience, *Nursing Forum, 46*, 269-279.

2. Brown, B. (2000). Men in nursing: Ambivalence in care, gender and masculinity, *International History of Nursing Journal, 5*, 4-13.
3. O'Lynn, C.E., & Tranbarger, R.E. (2007). *Men in nursing: History, challenges, and opportunities*, New York, NY: Springer Publishing Company.
4. Anthony, A.S. (2004). Gender bias and discrimination in nursing education: Can we change it?, *Nurse Educator, 29*, 121-125.
5. Men in Nursing: A Historical Timeline. Retrieved from http://allnurses.com/men-in-nursing/men-nursing-historical-96326.html
6. Evans, J. (2004). Men nurses: A historical and feminist perspective, *Journal of Advanced Nursing, 47*, 321-328.
7. Villeneuve, M.J. (1994). Recruiting and retaining men in nursing: A review of the literature, *Journal of Professional Nursing, 10*, 217-228.
8. Mackintosh, C. (1997). A historical study of men in nursing, *Journal of Advanced Nursing, 26*, 232-236.
9. Roth, J.E., & Coleman, C.L. (2008). Perceived and real barriers for men entering nursing: Implications for gender diversity, *Journal of Cultural Diversity, 15*(3), 148-152.
10. McLaughlin, K., Muldoon, O., & Moutray, M. (2010). Gender, gender roles and completion of nursing education: A longitudinal study, *Nurse Education Today, 30*, 303-307.
11. Kleinman, C.S. (2004). Understanding and capitalizing on men's advantages in nursing, *Journal of Nursing Administration, 34*(2), 78-82.
12. Evans, J. (1997). Men in nursing: Issues of gender segregation and hidden advantage, *Journal of Advanced Nursing, 26*, 226-231.
13. O'Lynn, C.E. (2004). Gender based barriers for male students in nursing education programs: Prevalence and perceived importance, *Journal of Nursing Education,* 43(5), 229-236.
14. Carol, R. (2006). Discrimination in nursing school: Thing of the past or alive and well? *Minority Nurse*, 56-62.
15. Anthony, A.S. (2004). Gender bias and discrimination in nursing education: Can we change it?, *Nurse Educator, 29*(3), 121-125.
16. Dyck, J.M., Oliffe, J., Phinney, A., & Garrett, B. (2009). Nursing instructors' and male students' perceptions of undergraduate, classroom nursing education, *Nurse Education Today, 29*, 649-653.
17. Harding, T. (2009). Swimming against the malestream: Men choosing nursing as a career, *Nursing Praxis in New Zealand, 25*(3), 4-16.
18. Harding, T., North, N., & Perkins, R. (2008). Sexualizing men's touch: Male nurses and the use of intimate touch in clinical practice, *Research and Theory for Nursing Practice: An International Journal, 22*(2), 88-101.
19. Eldredge, J. (2001). *Wild at heart: Discovering the secret of a man's soul*. Nashville, TN: Thomas Nelson.
20. Brady, M.S., & Sherrod, D.R. (2003). Retaining men in nursing programs designed for women, *Journal of Nursing Education, 42*(4), 159-162.
21. Keri, G. (2002). Male and female college students' learning styles differ: An opportunity for instructional diversification, *College Student Journal, 36*(3), 433.

Appendix C: Practical Preparation to Pass the NCLEX
1. Talking Points to the 2013 NCLEX-RN Passing Standard (2013). *NMBON*.sks.com. Retrieved from http://nmbon.sks.com/uploads/files/2013%20NCLEX-RN%20passing%20standard%20talking%20points.pdf
2. NCLEX-RN Test Plan (2013). *NCSBN*.org. Retrieved from https://www.ncsbn.org/2013_NCLEX_RN_Test_Plan.pdf

Appendix H
1. Vallerand, A.H., Sanoski, C.A., & Deglin, J.H. (2013) *Davis's drug guide for nurses*. (13th ed.). Philadelphia, PA: F.A. Davis Company.

Appendix L
1. Shah, A. Today, around 21,000 children died around the world. *GlobalIssues.*org. Retrieved May10, 2013 from http://www.globalissues.org/article/715/today-over-26,500-children-died-around-the-world.